Self-Help Kit

Small Claims

Guidance Manual

The contents of this Manual have been approved by Veronica Newman, barrister

Important Facts about this Lawpack Kit

This Lawpack Kit contains authoritative advice, instruction and the necessary forms for making a small claim.

This Lawpack Kit is only for people wishing to file a small claim in England or Wales. It is not suitable for Scotland or Northern Ireland.

The information it contains has been carefully compiled from professional sources but its accuracy is not guaranteed as laws and regulations may change or be subject to differing interpretations. The law is stated as at 1st September 2006.

Neither this nor any other publication can take the place of a solicitor on important legal matters.

This Lawpack Kit is sold with the understanding that the publisher, author and retailer are not engaged in rendering legal services. If legal advice or other expert assistance is required, the services of a competent professional should be sought.

As with any legal matter, common sense should determine whether you need the assistance of a solicitor rather than relying solely on the information and forms in this Lawpack Kit.

We strongly urge you to consult a solicitor if:

- substantial amounts of money are involved,
- you do not understand the instructions or are uncertain how to complete and use a form correctly, or
- what you want to do is not precisely covered by the forms provided.

For convenience (and for no other reason) 'him', 'he' and 'his' have been used throughout and should be read to include 'her', 'she' and 'her'.

EXCLUSION OF LIABILITY AND DISCLAIMER

Whilst every effort has been made to ensure that this Lawpack Kit provides accurate and expert guidance, it is impossible to predict all the circumstances in which it may be used. Accordingly, the publisher, author and retailer and the barrister who has approved the contents shall not be liable to any person or entity with respect to any loss or damage caused or alleged to be caused directly or indirectly by the information or any mistake contained in this Lawpack Kit.

Lawpack Kit gives you a limited guarantee. If you consider this Lawpack Kit to be defective or unsatisfactory in any way you may return it to us with your receipt within 30 days of the date of purchase for a full refund. In no event shall our liability exceed the purchase price of this Lawpack Kit. Use of this Lawpack Kit constitutes acceptance of these terms.

© 2006 Lawpack Publishing Limited
Crown copyright material is reproduced with the permission of the Controller of HMSO and the Queen's Printer for Scotland.

Contents

How to use this Kit	4
Before you file your small claims case	5
Winning without going to court	7
When your claim is disputed	11
Do you have a winning case?	12
Where to start proceedings	14
What you will have to pay	15
Who can bring a claim?	16
Who can be sued?	17
How much can you sue for?	19
How do you calculate the size of your claim?	19
Completing your small claims forms	22
Issuing your small claim	22
How the defendant is notified of the claim	23
After service	24
Winning your case	32
How to start proceedings online	36
Enforcing your judgment	37
Other useful remedies	40
Glossary of useful terms	43

Completed examples of loose-leaf forms contained in this Kit and on the free CD:

- Claim Form N1 — 46
- Certificate of Service Form N215 — 50
- Request for Judgment and Reply to Admission Form N225 — 56
- Request for Warrant of Execution Form N323 — 61
- Application Notice Form N244 — 62
- Application for Order that Debtor Attend Court for Questioning Form N316 — 64
- Application for Third Party Debt Order Form N349 — 66

Completed examples of loose-leaf forms sent by the Court – not included in this Kit:

- Notes for Claimant N1A — 48
- Defendant's Reply Form N9A (Admission) — 52
- Defendant's Reply Form N9B (Defence) — 54
- Allocation Questionnaire Form N149 — 57

How to use this Kit

This Lawpack Kit can help you achieve an important legal objective conveniently, efficiently and economically. Nevertheless it is important for you to use this Lawpack Kit properly if you are to avoid later difficulties.

- Read this Manual carefully. It contains the instructions you need to complete the documents in this Lawpack Kit. If after thorough examination you decide that your requirements are not met by this Lawpack Kit, or you do not feel confident about writing your own documents, then consult a solicitor.

- Forms can be photocopied as required. When completing your forms, do not leave any section blank. If any section is inapplicable, write 'not applicable' or 'none'. This shows you have not overlooked the section.

- Always use a pen or type on legal documents, never use a pencil.

- Do not cross out or erase anything you have written on your final forms.

- You will find a helpful glossary of terms at the end of this Manual. Refer to this glossary if you find unfamiliar terms.

This Lawpack Kit is 'web enabled', meaning it is supported on the web with extra information, updates and news on the subject covered. To access this, all you have to do is register on the Lawpack website at www.lawpack.co.uk/smallclaimskit, entering the code printed below when requested.

Registration code: **P2082690405**

Please note that this Kit is fully functional without the user having to register or use this service.

Before you file your small claims case

The Small Claims Track in the County courts is designed to be user-friendly, to encourage people to represent themselves in court for the purposes of pursuing simple claims for comparatively small sums. Judges are used to dealing with members of the public, hearings are less formal than in other courts and the normal rules of evidence do not apply.

The Civil Procedure Rules (CPR) govern how the court operates. This single set of rules covers both the High and County courts. Rule 1 sets out the Overriding Objective:

1.1 (1) These Rules are a new procedural code with the overriding objective of enabling the court to deal with cases justly.

  (2) Dealing with a case justly includes, so far as is practicable —
    (a) ensuring that the parties are on an equal footing;
    (b) saving expense;
    (c) dealing with the case in ways which are proportionate —
      (i) to the amount of money involved;
      (ii) to the importance of the case;
      (iii) to the complexity of the issues; and
      (iv) to the financial position of each party;
    (d) ensuring that it is dealt with expeditiously and fairly; and
    (e) allotting to it an appropriate share of the court's resources, while taking into account the need to allot resources to other cases.

The CPR are available at www.dca.gov.uk/civil/procrules_fin/menus/rules.htm.

All cases are now divided into one of three 'tracks', with different procedures adopted for each track.

1. Small Claims Track — Claims up to £5,000 (and see below).
2. Fast Track — Claims for £5,000–£15,000 with the trial to be no more than one day. (There are limited costs recovery rules and the trial will generally take place within 30 weeks of the case directions which are the orders the court makes for the administration of the case.)
3. Multi Track — Complex cases and claims over £15,000.

 ## What is the Small Claims Track?

It is a simplified procedure within the County court for dealing with claims for amounts of money under £5,000. It is not a separate court but is often called 'the Small Claims Court'.

The Small Claims Track covers the following types of case:

- Any claim which has a financial value of not more than £5,000.
- Any claim for personal injuries which has a financial value of not more than £5,000 where the claim for general damages for personal injuries is not more than £1,000.
- Any claim which includes a claim by a tenant of residential premises against his landlord for repairs or other work to the premises where the estimated cost of the repairs or other work is not more than £1,000 and the financial value of any claim for damages in respect of those repairs or other work is not more than £1,000.

Within the County court there are two types of judges:

1. Circuit Judges: these are the more senior and normally sit in a formal court room wearing wigs and gowns.
2. District Judges: these normally sit in a court room known as chambers and do not wear wigs and gowns. The parties sit around a table and the procedure is less formal.

Small claims are, except in special circumstances, dealt with by a District Judge not by a Circuit Judge.

Three advantages of the Small Claims Track:

1. You can prepare and present your case without having to pay a lawyer. A lawyer's fee will most likely be more than your claim. Under the Small Claims Track you have a chance of recovering the full amount of your loss with little or no costs. You can use a solicitor to represent you, but in most cases a solicitor is not necessary.
2. Making a small claim is a simple process.

   Because the Small Claims Track is so simple you should not need a solicitor. Within this Lawpack Kit are all the necessary forms you need to make a small claim. If you have any doubt a Consumer Advice Centre (e.g. the Community Legal Service at www.justask.org.uk) or a Citizens' Advice Bureau can be of great help.
3. A small claim is a speedy process.

   Most small claims cases are heard within a few months of sending a claim form to the court.

What can you sue for using the Small Claims Track?

You cannot sue for an amount larger than £5,000 using the Small Claims Track in the County court. If you believe you are entitled to more than £5,000 you can voluntarily lower your claim to £5,000 so you can use the Small Claims Track. This may be advisable, for instance, if you think you have a claim for £5,200. Here it may be wiser to sacrifice the additional £200 for recovery without legal fees. The £5,000 limit does not include any sum you claim for interest under the County Courts Act 1984 (see pages 19/20).

Virtually any type of claim (under £5,000 if seeking money damages) can be brought as a small claim. The following are some typical small claims matters:

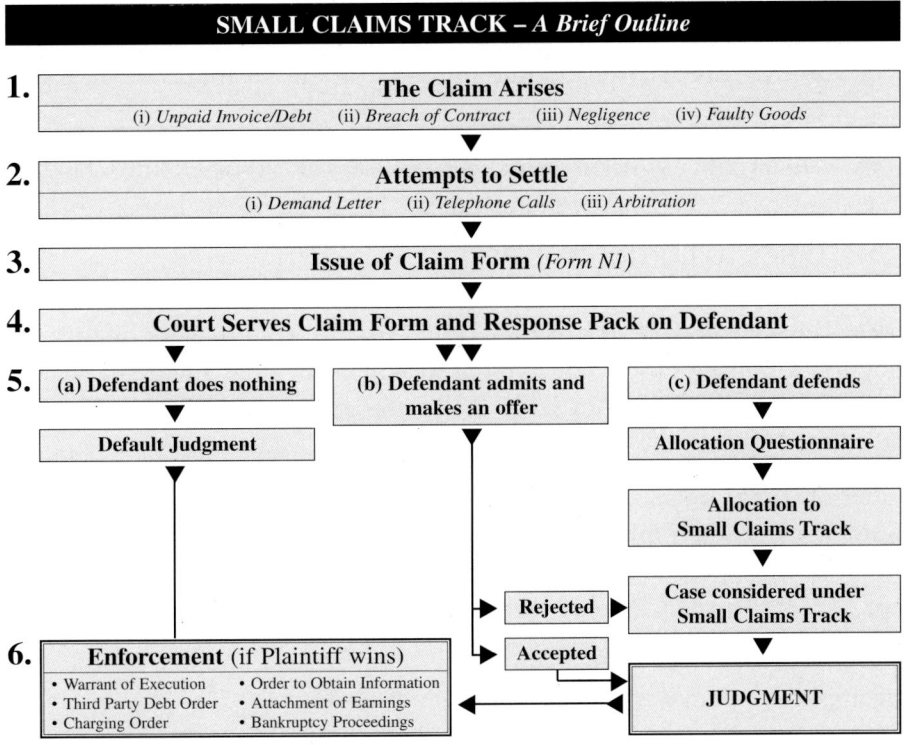

- Debt collection
- Landlord/tenant actions
- Personal injury cases
- Property damage
- Disputes over services rendered
- Contract disputes

You cannot use the Small Claims Track in the County court for possession proceedings.

Any claim can be taken out of the Small Claims Track if the court decides the issues involved are too complex.

Winning without going to court

How do you win in court? One short answer is to avoid it. You can be a winner by resolving your dispute before you enter court. Litigation should be the last resort. The judicial system should be used only when all other alternatives fail. Why?

- Courts take time
- Courts involve costs
- Courts involve risk

Before you issue proceedings, ask yourself if you have done everything reasonably possible to settle with the other party.

This Lawpack Kit will show you how best to win in court once you decide that the Small Claims Track is your only remedy. But winning in court is not easy. You may lose or you may not recover the full amount you are seeking. You may also have difficulty collecting your judgment.

Therefore, make every effort to settle your claim before going to court. Here is how:

Step 1. Offer to compromise

Contact the person you are having trouble with. Try to work matters out. A willingness to compromise is not a sign of weakness but a sign of intelligence. A small compromise may allow you to settle the matter right away. People often refuse to settle matters because they have never been asked to. Ask!

An offer of compromise, made either orally or in writing, does not bind you to that amount if the compromise is not accepted. But your correspondence should be marked 'without prejudice.' For example, if you tell your adversary that you will accept £1,500 of the £1,750 you feel is due, you can still issue proceedings for the original £1,750 if the offer is rejected.

Some important points about 'without prejudice' offers:

- You can offer to accept less without the other party using such an offer against you in court as long as you mark the offer 'without prejudice.' It is designed to encourage parties to reach a settlement.
- No correspondence can be shown to the District Judge if it is an offer to settle and is 'without prejudice.'
- If the other party accepts your 'without prejudice' offer then that is a contract and both parties are bound by it.

Once you reach a compromise, put your agreement in writing. This way avoids confusion about the terms of your oral agreement, and you will have proof of the settlement if there are any later problems in collecting.

If you cannot reach a compromise, also put this in writing. This will show your good faith in attempting to settle rather than going to court. Some judges appreciate this effort.

Step 2. First demand letter

If you fail to compromise, your next step is to send your adversary a letter.

There are three reasons why a demand letter is essential:

1. It is useful in trying to settle your dispute.
2. You can use it as evidence in court, and it is a good way of outlining your case before the judge.
3. You will have complied with the overriding objective under the Civil Procedure Rules.

The sole purpose of a demand letter is to resolve the problem. Write your letter tactfully. Do not alienate the other party. Be firm but polite. For instance, if you own a business, your letter should gently remind a forgetful debtor of his overdue bill. There is no need to be hostile.

Your demand letter should be brief and set out the relevant facts of the dispute. Present your case logically. Write the letter so that it briefly reviews the entire dispute. Include in your letter your reply to any points the other party is likely to make. It may seem odd to recite facts to someone who already knows them but you are not really just writing to your adversary. The judge may eventually see your letter. So you want to state your position in a way the judge can most easily understand it. Remember, the judge does not know how your problem started or developed. Your letter may be the only way the judge becomes familiar with your position.

This is also important because the District Judge will most likely see this letter at the outset of the case and so will be familiar with your argument first. If the other party never sets out his case in writing this increases your chance of success.

Your demand letter must say that if you do not get satisfaction, you will go to court. Set a time limit for resolution but do not threaten. When setting time limits always make them clearly identifiable, i.e. seven days from the date of this letter. Make the issuing of a claim form your last resort.

Send two copies of your demand letter, one by first-class post and one by registered post so you can prove your letter was received. Keep several copies of your demand letter. You will need to bring them to court with you. Always give the judge a copy of your letter as part of your case. It is sometimes a good idea to enclose a complete but unissued copy of your small claims summons form to show that you are serious.

Sometimes a debtor will be happy to reach a compromise settlement for less than the full amount. You too may feel that it is wiser to cut your losses and settle; but consider these three factors before you settle:

1. The strength of your case.
2. The amount of time you are willing to spend on the case.
3. The amount of money you are willing to spend on the case.

If you settle your case after you have issued your claim form in the County court but before the hearing, make sure your settlement is in writing. Advise the court that you will not appear at your hearing. If your settlement involves payment by instalments, go to court and present your agreement to the judge. You can have a judgment entered that complies with your settlement agreement. This way, if the judgment is not paid, you can use the collection methods discussed further in this Lawpack Kit. If you have issued a claim form, never tell the court to discontinue your claim until you have been paid in full

Step 3. Telephone calls

A telephone call is an alternative way of settling your claim. Calls can produce positive results because they are difficult to ignore, and often people may be more inclined to work out some type of payment arrangement there and then.

Some people find it very difficult to face up to a problem. It is easy to ignore correspondence, it is not so easy to ignore telephone calls. People are very often relieved to settle an outstanding problem.

Speaking to your adversary may also help to resolve the matter amicably by giving them a chance to voice their reasons for not paying you. But to succeed your telephone calls must be reasonable and businesslike, not harassing or abusive.

Telephone calls require planning and preparation. Here are some steps to follow:

- **Be organised.** Make sure you have everything in front of you necessary to discuss your claim, and review it one more time before you make the call.
- **Identify yourself.** State your name and the reason for your call. If you are calling on behalf of a business, state your name, your title, and the name of the business.
- **Speak only to the debtor.** Or the person in charge of handling your claim.
- **Give introductory information.** Including:
    1. The claim you are referring to.
    2. The exact amount owed.
    3. When the debt was incurred.
    4. How much time the debtor has had to pay.

Step 4. Use successful settlement methods

To get paid without making a small claim requires some basic understanding of the collection methods that do work. Here are a few pointers:

- **Start by demanding payment in full.** Do not indicate that you may accept instalment or partial payments. Insist upon immediate full payment of the debt. The debtor will undoubtedly give reasons why you are not entitled to full payment or offer excuses for non-payment.
- **Encourage the debtor to make the first offer of settlement.** It may be for more than you would have been willing to accept.
- **Negotiate for instalments.** Often debtors simply do not have the money to pay all at once, although they could perhaps pay in instalments. Do reach precise agreement on how much will be paid and when. Obviously, you should try to get as much as possible on the first payment.

    If agreeing to instalments, always get the first payment immediately. Debtors will often agree to a payment schedule but never pay when the time comes. This results in unnecessary delay.

    If you reach agreement on a payment schedule, always make it a condition that if any payment is not made on a due date the full amount becomes due immediately.

- **Try for security.** Will the debtor offer security? Protect yourself in case the debtor later defaults on the promise to pay.
- **Request that the problem be resolved.** If what you want is specific action rather than money, ask for it. For example, if you want the company to fix your roof properly, say so. Make sure you direct your request to the person in charge of making decisions for the business and who can give you what you want.

- **Make the settlement sound appealing.** When a dispute is settled, there are savings on both sides. The creditor saves the time and expense of litigation. The debtor saves his credit rating and court costs. Make these advantages clear to your adversary.
- **Send a confirming letter.** Refer to your discussions and any verbal agreement and outline all the points. Stress the date you expect payment.
- **Does the debtor belong to some type of association or professional body?** If so contact them and check if there is any way they can help bring pressure on the debtor. For instance, the Association of Independent Tour Operators (tel: 020 8744 9280 or www.aito.co.uk) operates a system of low cost arbitration over complaints against one of its members. Check the terms of any written agreement. See later for the benefits of arbitration.
- **Ignore lame excuses.** Is the debtor's cheque in the post? If this is the first time you have heard this story, give your debtor the benefit of the doubt and say you will wait one week to receive it.

Did the debtor lose his job? Suggest a modest repayment schedule until the debtor is employed again. But do verify the debtor's story.

A divorce? This has no effect upon your claim. Whoever was obliged to pay you before the divorce is still obliged after the divorce, whatever agreement exists between the spouses.

When you feel you can no longer work things out with your adversary you must leave them with four thoughts:

1. The importance of paying the bill.
2. The bill is overdue.
3. You will carry on with the process until the bill is paid.
4. They can work with you now or pay a judgment with interest and court costs later.

When your claim is disputed

In most instances the debtor knows they owe you the money, but due to financial hardship have not the money to pay. Patience and a repayment schedule can usually resolve these cases.

Still, there are times when people have *bona fide* disputes. Was the roof properly fixed? Did the neighbour cause the damage to the fence? Is the dress you had made a proper fit?

If you and your adversary cannot reach agreement on your own, you may wish to consider an alternative to the Small Claims Track.

There is a growing number of trade organisations that run dispute resolution processes. It could be your adversary is a member of a trade body that has such a process. For example, the British Dental Council has implemented a scheme by which complaints panels hear disputes between dental health practitioners and private patients (for more information visit www.dentalcomplaints.org.uk). The Association of Master Upholsterers and Soft Furnishers also has a dispute resolution process it offers to dissatisfied customers of its members (for more information visit www.upholsterers.com). The list of trade bodies that offer dispute resolution is growing, so it is worth finding out whether there is one that might assist you.

Mediation

Mediation is a way for people to settle their disputes by discussing them with the help of a trained mediator, and some County courts now offer a separate mediation service. The idea is to get all the parties to reach an agreement. If you cannot afford a court scheme or your local court does not yet have a scheme for mediation, you may be able to get your dispute mediated through the Law Works Mediation Scheme (LWMS). The Law Centres Federation and the Solicitors Pro Bono Group set up Law Works to co-ordinate and deliver free ('pro-bono') legal help to clients of Law Centres and Citizens' Advice Bureaux. However, courts do refer people who have begun claims in the small claims court to Law Works. To access the service go to www.probonogroup.org.uk/mediation; or email mediate@probonogroup.org.uk; or write to: The Administrators, Law Works Mediation Scheme, 1 Pudding Lane, London EC3R 8AB

To be considered for help you must complete an application form giving details of the dispute and the efforts that have been made to resolve it. In suitable cases, where the client cannot pay for the service and no legal aid is available an accredited mediator from LWMS's panel of mediators will be appointed. The mediator's services are free.

There are three advantages to mediation:

1. As an alternative to presenting your case to a judge as part of an adversarial process, you decide the outcome, with the other side, aided by a court-appointed mediator.
2. It is faster to see a mediator right away than to wait your turn to have your case heard in the Small Claims Court.
3. If both parties cannot agree, you can still go to court and have a judge hear your case.

The Department for Constitutional affairs is keen to promote mediation, so your local court or even the district judge hearing your case may suggest mediation. However, at the moment the process is voluntary and you do not have to agree to mediation. If you do wish to try mediation the court will suggest the National Mediation Helpline, www.nationalmediationhelpline.com, on 0845 60 30 809. The Helpline can put you in touch with a range of mediation providers, each of which is a member of the Civil Mediation Council and Helpline-accredited. From 1st August 2006 the cost of a mediation for a claim of less than £5,000 is £100 plus VAT for two hours.

If mediation fails, you may find that the Small Claims Track is your only resort.

Do you have a winning case?

Before you go to court you must resolve three issues:

1. Can you win your case?
2. Can you collect on your judgment?
3. Can the court hear your case?

What makes a winning case? Liability. You will not get any money from a defendant until you prove that the defendant is legally responsible for your loss. This means that you must prove liability. Your loss is not enough to make a winning case, it must also be the other side's legal fault. You must state facts to the judge to show that the defendant should be held legally accountable.

The judge will listen to your evidence and decide whether you have a legal case. Having a legal case means you have a legal right to claim compensation from your debtor or the wrongdoer – lawyers call this having 'a cause of action'. It is for you to establish the facts in as favourable a way as possible and for the judge to rule on the legal position. However, if you understand some of the principles of the relevant law, it will aid your preparation and help ensure your arguments are more easily understood and appreciated by the judge. This should lead to a better chance of success.

Look at the following examples:

- **Contract dispute.** A valid contract signed by both parties has been broken by the other side and you have suffered monetary loss (e.g. an invoice has not been paid). The contract does not have to be a written one. It can be a verbal agreement.
- **Negligence.** Negligence means a wrongful act or failure to act has occurred. For example, someone cuts down a tree which falls on your car. You are entitled to claim compensation for the cost of putting right the damage to your car.
- **Personal injury.** The intentional or negligent behaviour of the defendant has caused you to suffer personal injury (e.g. a road accident).
- **Defective product.** You suffered loss due to a defective product and have the right of compensation from the person who supplied it and/or the manufacturer.
- **Warranties.** A written or implied warranty or guarantee has been breached and you have suffered a monetary loss.
- **Consumer claim.** If you are an individual and bought goods or services from a business that proved to be defective or wrong, your case may be covered by consumer legislation such as the Sale of Goods and Services Acts. These have specific rules relating to such claims that make it easier to prove them. For more information visit www.consumerdirect.gov.uk.

 ## Can you collect on your judgment?

It is most important that you can show that the defendant's wrongful act caused you actual injury which can be translated into a monetary recovery. Wrongdoing without harm is not usually compensatable.

Even if you win, your victory is worthless unless you can enforce the judgment. If your defendant is genuinely unable to pay, they may not be worth chasing and they may not even defend themselves.

Unfortunately, there is no simple way to investigate the finances of a defendant unless you are prepared to pay for an asset search, but this is seldom cost-effective in a small claims case. At best you can only make casual enquiries to learn what you can about the defendant. You may find they have many more creditors, some of whom hold judgments ahead of yours.

It is important to be practical. It makes no more sense to waste valuable time, effort, and court costs chasing an uncollectable debt than it does suing on a negligible claim.

The Small Claims Track only makes sense when you have a reasonable chance of winning and collecting enough money to make the exercise worthwhile.

Can the court hear your case?

The courts can only hear cases where the law of England and Wales apply. If you purchased goods abroad the law which applies is nearly always the law of the country in which the purchase was made. Sometimes the contract will state which law applies. For example, if you purchase computer software over the internet the contract will state which law applies.

Where to start proceedings

Small claims cases are always dealt with in a County court. You can start your claim in any County court. However, the proceedings will be transferred to the defendant's local court if:

- the defendant is an individual; and
- you are claiming a fixed sum of money, such as a debt; and
- the defendant replies to the court stating that he will defend the claim.
- you began the claim using 'Money Claim Online' (see page 36) and the defendant has decided to oppose your claim

In these cases the transfer is automatic and you will be notified by the new court once your claim is transferred to them.

If your claim is for compensation 'damages', i.e. where you cannot immediately say how much is claimed, as in a personal injury case, then the claim will not be transferred.

It is best to keep proceedings in your own court, particularly if the defendant lives some way away.

How do you find a County court? They are located throughout the country, and you can find one near you, or the defendant, by referring to the telephone directory under 'Courts'. The courts are open Monday to Friday from 10 a.m. to 4 p.m. Alternatively, visit www.courtservice.gov.uk where there is a list of court addresses.

What you will have to pay

There is a fee required to start a small claims case so it is important to have confidence of recovery before you issue proceedings.

For non-monetary claims the fee is £150, but for money claims the exact amount you will be required to pay will depend upon the amount of your claim. At present, the fees for a claim are as follows:

Amount claimed	County court fee	Money Claim Online fee
up to £300	£30	£20
up to £500	£50	£40
up to £1,000	£80	£70
up to £5,000	£120	£110

Since the fees do change, it is best to have the court staff advise you what your fee will be when you issue. The defendant will be ordered to pay this fee if you win but remember that you still have to recover the money from the defendant.

Recoverable costs

You can recover the following costs if you win your case:

- The fees paid to issue the case, for lodging an Allocation Questionnaire and for any applications to the court.
- If you used a solicitor to issue the case or to help you, the fixed costs for issuing. Currently these are between £50 and £80 depending upon how much you recover.
- Any witness expenses, such as for travel, and loss of earnings limited to £50 per day per witness.
- The costs of enforcing your judgment, if the debtor fails to pay.

Apart from filing fees and possible solicitor fees, you may also incur witness expenses. This is necessary if a witness is needed to corroborate your story, testify as to events or give an expert opinion. You must at least pay their reasonable travel expenses to and from the court and also any lost wages. If you or your witness has taken annual leave to give evidence, the court may order the losing side to pay compensation for loss of that annual leave. Expert witnesses will often expect a professional fee for their opinion and this may easily exceed any possible recovery from the case. If you use an expert, you can only recover £200 for his or her fees if you win.

Remember the case can be transferred by the judge out of the Small Claims Track to the Fast or Multi Tracks in circumstances where the judge feels it is too complex, legally or factually. If this happens, from that date onward the winning party can recover the legal costs of instructing a solicitor.

It is worth checking your household insurance if you are considering starting a small claim; some policies include legal expenses insurance.

If you lose your case, can the court order you to pay the defendant's costs?

Apart from the cost of the claim form issue fee, the court rules do not permit a defendant or a claimant to claim costs against the other unless he has behaved unreasonably. What amounts to 'unreasonable behaviour' is a matter for the District Judge. Examples of unreasonable behaviour might include:

- pursuing a hopeless, as opposed to a weak, case for the purpose of embarrassing the defendant;
- requesting a fresh hearing date at the last minute, because the other party has not prepared the case;
- making a dishonest claim;
- deliberately misstating the value of a claim to avoid a transfer to the Fast Track.

However, like a successful claimant, a defendant who 'wins' the case by resisting a claim may ask the court for:

- his own, or his witnesses', loss of earnings or loss of annual leave due to attending a hearing or staying away from home for the purpose of attending a hearing, limited to £50 per person per day
- the cost of an expert's fees, limited to £200 per expert

Remember such awards of costs are discretionary. The District Judge is not obliged to award costs unless he considers it is appropriate.

Conditional fees – personal injury cases

Solicitors are now allowed to act for clients on a conditional or 'no win, no fee' basis in personal injury cases. This means that if you win the case you pay them their normal costs plus a 'success fee'; if you lose the case you pay nothing. The success fee varies; at most it can be double the amount of normal costs, but cannot be based upon the solicitor taking a percentage of the compensation. Remember that if you lose you may still have to pay the other side's fees if you are not within the small claims limit.

What if you cannot afford the court fees?

If you cannot afford to pay the court fees you may be entitled to a remission (reduction) of the fees payable or you may be exempted from having to pay them at all. Ask your County court office for form EX160A or visit www.hmcourts-service.gov.uk to find out if you qualify for this help.

Who can bring a claim?

If you are making a claim you are the claimant. The party you are suing is the defendant. There can be multiple claimants and multiple defendants.

Any individual over the age of 18 can make a claim. A young person ('minor') under the age of 18 can only claim on his or her own behalf for unpaid wages. A minor can file a claim through a guardian or a parent. Always state your full name, do not use initials.

You may, as a business owner or operator, also make a claim.

- If you are a firm, then make a claim as a firm using its name, followed by the words 'a firm'. You would then list the address of the firm. Example: Lawpack Publishing, a firm, 76-89 Alscot Road, London, SE1.
- If you are a limited company use its name designation 'limited company' and either its trading address or the address of its registered office. Example: Lawpack Publishing Limited, a limited company, 76-89 Alscot Road, London, SE1.
- If you are a person doing business under another name, use your own name followed by the words 'trading as', and the address of the business. Example: John Smith trading as Lawpack Publishing, 76-89 Alscot Road, London, SE1.

Who can be sued?

You can sue just about anyone.

Always take care to consider who you name on the summons. If you get the wrong party, then the claim may be struck out and costs ordered against you. If in doubt seek advice from the court, or a Citizens' Advice Bureau.

The following are general rules on whom you can sue.

Suing one person

If you are suing an individual, name the individual using the most complete name that you have for that person.

Suing two or more people

If you are suing more than one person on a claim arising from the same incident, list and serve each of them. For example, if you are suing John Doe and John Smith for the £1,000 they borrowed from you, list them as follows: 'John Doe and John Smith.' This is also required for a husband and wife. Do not list them as Mr. and Mrs. Smith. Additionally, each defendant must be served separately. Service of process will be discussed in a later section.

If you are suing more than one person on two claims, you must sue each one in a separate action under the Small Claims Track.

Suing a sole trader

If you are suing a sole trader, list the name of the owner and the name of the business. This would be as follows: 'Jo Bloggs trading as ABC Painting'.

Make sure you know who the true owner of the business is before you sue. A judgment against an incorrect defendant is worth very little.

Suing a firm

If you are suing a partnership, you have a choice of either suing the individual partners or the partnership itself.

The advantages of suing the partnership are that:

- service is easier and the proceedings are simpler;
- judgment can be enforced without special permission of the judge (i.e. without leave) against partnership property;
- judgment can be enforced without leave against the personal property of any person who was identified as a partner in the proceedings.

All partners are individually liable for all the debts of the business, so you need not specify which partner you dealt with particularly.

List the partnership as follows: 'ABC Painting, a firm' followed by the address. Try to get a judgment against more than one person so if you have trouble collecting from one you may have others to collect from.

 Suing a limited company

If you are suing a limited company, list its full name and address. Example: 'ABC Painting, Ltd. a limited company, 76-89 Alscot Road, London, SE1'.

A limited company is considered by English law to be a person (it has a 'corporate personality'). This means that you can sue and enforce a judgment against a company. Do not sue the owners of the limited company or its managing director individually unless you have a personal claim against them that is separate from their role as part of the limited company. Most of the time people who own or operate a limited company are usually not liable for its corporate debts. This is known as limited liability and is what makes forming a limited company so important.

 Suing a club or association

If you are suing a club or association, such as a football or rugby club, you must list the names of the officers of the club or association. For example, 'Deborah Brown in her capacity as Chairman of the Dowl Association of Junior Swimmers' and 'Ian Trot in his capacity as Secretary of the Dowl Association of Junior Swimmers'. You would also need to obtain the home addresses of the officers, as they have to be served by the court at their home addresses; these can be obtained by writing to the Secretary of the club or association.

 Suing a child

While anyone under 18 cannot sue by themselves (except for wages), they can be sued. If your defendant is a child, i.e. under 18, you should specify this as follows: 'James Smith, a child by *[insert name of parent currently responsible for him/her]* … his/her litigation friend'. It would be wise to check whether the parents have legal responsibility for the acts or debts of the child. If they do, they should also be named as defendants.

How much can you sue for?

You cannot sue for more than £5,000 using the Small Claims Track. If your claim exceeds that amount you must either reduce your claim or else bring your action in another track. You are not allowed just to divide a claim that is over the £5,000 limit into two or more claims so that each is within the limit. For example, X lent Y £6,000. Y was to repay X in two instalments, each for £3,000. X cannot argue that there were two separate contracts. The loan was one transaction; X may not have two claims heard in the court using the Small Claims Track.

How do you calculate the size of your claim?

When in doubt, overestimate slightly. If you are unsure as to the exact amount of your claim, always issue your action for damages a little higher than you believe they are worth. This is because the judge has the power to award you less than you request, but will never award you more.

If you find yourself in court and realise you have asked for too little, request that the judge allow you to amend your claim. If the judge allows this, your case may be continued at a later date.

It is easy to work out the exact amount you are entitled to. The following are some examples of how the exact amount of a claim may be calculated:

Contract disputes

To arrive at the exact figure for a contract claim, work out the difference between the amount you were supposed to receive under the contract and what you actually received. For example, if 'A' was to paint 'B''s house for £1,000, and 'B' only paid 'A' £750, 'A' has a claim against 'B' for £250.

Interest

You can claim interest on all moneys which are due to you whether your claim is for a fixed amount or damages to be assessed.

Interest rates

- If you have a contract which specifies how interest is charged then you can rely upon this.
- Otherwise all debts carry interest at the judgment rate which is currently eight per cent per annum.
- Damages, once assessed, are awarded interest at a rate the judge decides is reasonable.
- If you are a business, you are entitled to claim interest under the Late Payment of Commercial Debts (Interest) Act 1998 – for more information about this, visit www.payontime.co.uk

How interest is calculated

- Claim from the date the debt became due. If it became due over a period of time then you can either stagger it or simply calculate on the whole sum from the date the last amount became due.

- Interest continues to be due up until the date of your judgment or until payment is made if this is before any judgment. It does not carry on after judgment unless the amount of the judgment is over £5,000. For example, Stephanie owes Jane £800 for making a wedding dress. Jane's bill is dated 26th February 2006. Stephanie fails to pay and makes weak excuses until Jane's patience is exhausted. Jane completes the claim form N1 on 25th May 2006. Jane claims interest at 8 per cent per annum under the County Courts Act 1984. Jane needs to work out the daily rate of interest on the debt. She starts by working out the annual interest by multiplying £800 by 8 and dividing by 100.

  800 x 8 = 6,400

  6,400 divided by 100 = 64

  Jane works out the daily rate of interest:

  64 divided by 365 days = 0.175

  round it up to 18 pence per day.

  There are 89 days between the date of Jane's bill and the date she completes the N1; 89 x 18 pence per day is £16.02. Therefore Jane needs to claim £800, plus £16.02 from the date of the debt being due until the date she completes her N1, and a further 18 pence for each day after the date on the N1 until the date of judgment or payment, whichever is sooner.

You must enter the claim for interest together with the sum you are claiming in the 'Amount claimed' box on the N1 claim form.

Also make sure that your damages include only the amount of money you are owed. In other words, do not try to collect money in court that you have already recovered from someone else.

Property damage

The exact amount of your claim for property damage is usually the amount of money it would take to fix the damaged item. For example, if A's car was dented by B, A would sue B for the amount it would cost to repair it. To be safe, A should get several estimates.

If the cost to repair the damaged item exceeds the value of the item, you may only be entitled to the value of the item. If the cost to fix A's dented car exceeds the market value of A's car before the accident, A may only be entitled to sue B for the market value of the car. This will depend upon other factors such as whether the item is easily replaceable.

If you are only entitled to the fair market value of the item, you must deduct the value of the object after the injury. If the fair market value of A's car is £3,000 and it would cost £3,200 to repair the dent, A may sue for £3,000 (the value of the car). However, the value of the car **after** the dent must be deducted from that amount. If A's car is now worth £500 with the dent, that amount must be deducted from the

£3,000 fair market value of A's car. This means A's damages are £2,500.

Think of it this way: if the cost of repair exceeds the value of the object, you are likely to be limited to the fair market value of the object, less the value of the object after damage.

Do not forget though, if the value of the damaged object exceeds the cost of repair, you are entitled to sue for the cost of the repair. If A's car is worth £5,000 and the dent cost £500 to repair, A's claim is for £500.

Be prepared to show the actual value of your property in court. How do you do this? The best way is to get estimates from experts in the field and have these experts come to court and testify. Alternatively, they can put the value of your property in writing. You may also want to check newspaper ads for the prices asked for comparable goods. Proving your case in court will be discussed later.

In summary, to calculate the amount of your claim work out:

1. What the value was of the item before the accident.
2. How much it will cost to repair.
3. What the item is worth now it is damaged.

If 2 is less than 1, claim for 2. If 2 is more than 1, claim for 1 minus 3.

Damage to clothing

Claims involving clothing damage are different from other property damage cases because:

1. The Small Claims Track is frequently used in cases involving clothing.
2. Your own items of clothing have little value to anyone else, even if in good condition.

If your damaged clothing was new or almost new, sue for its cost. For example, if your dry-cleaners damaged your new £200 suit, sue for £200.

If your clothing was not new, sue for the percentage of value of the clothing which reflects how worn it was when the damage occurred. For example, your dry-cleaners damaged your suit which cost £200 two years ago. You have been wearing the suit fairly regularly and feel it would have lasted another two years. Since the suit had lost half of its useable life, you should sue for £100.

Personal injury cases

Few personal injury cases go to the Small Claims Court because the amount of the claims are usually much higher than the £1,000 small claims limit for personal injury. However, small personal injury cases do make it to the Small Claims Track.

To work out the exact amount of your personal injury claim, also consider:

1. Out-of-pocket expenses, such as fares to and from hospital appointments.
2. Loss of pay or vacation time for missing work.

3. Damage to property.
4. Pain and suffering (will be assessed by the judge).

Remember, you cannot collect money in court that you have already recovered from someone else. If your employer paid you for the days you missed work, do not expect to recover lost wages, or if you have received any state benefits these must be disclosed and taken into account.

The small claims limits for personal injury cases are different, because it is recognised that they often take more work and involve greater costs to prove the claim, especially so for medical reports, which are largely unrecoverable in small claims.

For this reason a personal injury matter can only be dealt with as a small claim where the total claim is less than £5,000 and of that no more than £1,000 is sought for general damages to your person, for example, if you claimed £2,000 for loss of earnings, £250 for damage to your clothing and £1,000 for a broken leg.

Be prepared to provide the judge with receipts as proof of your out-of-pocket expenses, such as medical bills, fares for visiting hospital, etc.

If you decide to claim over the personal injury limits, there are special rules that apply to personal injury matters and you should consult a Citizens' Advice Bureau or a solicitor.

Pain and suffering

Pain and suffering is the discomfort and inconvenience caused as a result of your injury. The court calculates the amount of damages by considering other cases of a similar nature.

Completing your small claims forms

It is not difficult to start a claim using the Small Claims Track. You will be shown how to complete the necessary forms in the remainder of this Manual. The claim form also has some helpful notes (N1A) to assist court users to complete the form. You will also find the court staff most helpful, as are the Consumer Advice Centres and the Citizens' Advice Bureaux. You will need three copies of the Claim Form (Form N1). This form is in this Lawpack Kit and is also available free from the County court. You can also print copies from the Courts Service website: **www.hmcourts-service.gov.uk/courtfinder/forms**. One copy is for the defendant, one for the court and one for yourself. If there is more than one defendant you will need an additional copy of the form for each additional defendant. See page 46 for an example of a completed Claim Form.

Issuing your small claim

Once you have fully completed your Form N1 you will need to give it to the court staff together with a fee (which varies in relation to the amount of your claim). You can either attend in person to start ('issue') proceedings or send it by post.

You will be sent in return a receipt for your fee called a Notice of Issue Form N205A. This also gives you your case number so you must keep this document carefully.

You have now started ('issued') the proceedings and the next step is to 'serve' the summons on the defendant. Serve is a legal term that means the defendant is notified of the claim.

How the defendant is notified of the claim

The defendant must be served with a copy of the Claim Form (Form N1) you have issued, along with the Response Pack Form N9 which the court sends. The Response Pack includes forms N9A, N9B, N9C and N9D (forms N9C and N9D are used where the claim is for an unspecified amount or it is not a claim for money). Forms N9A and N9B are for the defendant to admit the amount claimed in full or part and, if necessary, put a proposal for how he is to pay any moneys that are admitted, and state his defence. See pages 50 and 52 for examples.

Who can serve?

You have two choices as to how the claim form is served on the defendant.

1. The court can be asked to serve it on the defendant, which they will do by first-class post.
2. You can arrange to serve the defendant personally either yourself, by using a firm of process servers or any other person.

How do you serve?

There are four principal options available to you for service.

1. Personally serve the defendant by handing the claim form and the reply forms to him.
2. By first-class post to the defendant.
3. By leaving it at the last known address of the defendant.
4. Send the reply forms and claim form to the defendant's solicitor if the defendant has already instructed one and if the solicitor has agreed to accept service of the claim form.

It is also possible to serve by fax provided that you have the defendant's agreement to do so and the fax number to which it is to be sent. Both the agreement and the fax number must be in writing from the defendant.

Service by e-mail is only available where both sides have legal representatives acting for them.

If you serve the defendant yourself, you must send a Certificate of Service Form N215 (see completed example on page 48) to the court within seven days of service on the defendant.

It is best to leave service to the court, unless there is some degree of urgency or you believe the defendant will try to avoid being served with the claim form. The court sometimes takes a couple of weeks to serve the claim form, but by leaving it to the court you have less risk of making a mistake in the service which may ultimately result in delays. The court rules relating to service can be complex and their interpretation strict.

Defendant's time limits to respond

Once the claim form is served strict time limits come into play which all parties must comply with. The first of these is the time allowed for the defendant to return one of the options from the Response Pack N9. If the defendant fails to return the forms within the time limit then you can enter judgment in default.

Firstly, let us consider when the court rules deem that the defendant has received the claim form.

If the court is serving the defendant, it will note on the Notice of Issue Form N205A the date of service, which is deemed to be two days after the date of posting.

If you are serving yourself, then service is deemed as follows:

- If handed to the defendant — the time at which it was handed to them.
- If sent by post — the second day after posting.
- If left at an address — the day after delivery to the address.
- If by fax — if on a business day before 4.00 p.m. that day, otherwise the next business day.

It is possible the defendant will not receive your claim form. If the defendant moved, or you gave the incorrect address, the Post Office will return the claim form to the sender. If it was serving for you, the court will advise you of this by sending you a Notice of Non-Service Form N216 and ask you to effect service.

Unless you deliver the claim form to the defendant within four months from when you issued your claim you must seek permission from the court to extend the time for service. This is ordinarily granted when the court believes you are making a diligent effort to find the defendant.

Alternatively, you may withdraw your claim 'without prejudice', allowing you time to locate the defendant and issue your claim again.

After service

The defendant has five options once the claim form is received:

1. Attempt to settle the claim.
2. Admit owing you the money.
3. Admit owing some of the money claimed.
4. Deny owing you any money.
5. Ignore the claim form.

Let us examine each situation:

 ## The defendant wants to settle

This happens in a good many cases. Unfortunately, it may take a summons to be issued before a defendant realises you are serious about collecting. Many people will call your bluff and ignore you until the summons arrives, at which point they can no longer afford to ignore you.

Should the defendant approach you to settle, then you can follow the suggestions on pages 10 and 11, but perhaps take a more robust approach. After all, you have already started your proceedings and your settlement should reflect the inconvenience and costs involved.

After a defence has been returned to the court (Form N9A for money claims or Form N9C for non-monetary claims), when returning the Allocation Questionnaire (see page 27 for information on its purpose), the parties may request a one month stay in the proceedings to allow for a settlement to be agreed. The court can order such a stay if both parties ask for it or if the court considers it is appropriate. The purpose of this is simply to focus the parties' minds on settlement now before a hearing is listed.

 ## The defendant admits to owing you the money

This is a less common occurrence. When it does happen the defendant knows he has no valid defence to the claim and usually just needs time to pay the claim.

Here the defendant will complete Form N9A (admission), which is received together with the claim form. The defendant then sends the admission directly to you rather than the court.

Focus on question number 11 on the form. Invariably the defendant will propose a repayment schedule to pay the debt. You now have three choices:

a. Accept the defendant's payment proposal

Simply ask the court to send the defendant an order to pay you the proposed instalments. This is called 'entering judgment on acceptance.'

This is done by completing the Request for Judgment on the lower portion of the Notice of Issue Form N205A, which is then sent to the court. The court uses the information on Form N205A to complete the judgment order.

b. Say how you want the defendant to pay

If the defendant admits owing you money but has not proposed how to pay the debt, you can ask for the judgment to be paid in instalments or in one payment on Form N205A.

c. Refuse the defendant's offer to pay

To object to the defendant's payment proposal you must state on the lower portion of the back of Form N205A why you object and what you would be willing to accept. Return this to the court which will then review the defendant's proposal and your reply and decide how the defendant will pay. This is called 'entering a judgment by determination', which will be noted on Form N30(2) Judgment for Claimant, which will be sent to you and the defendant.

You are not bound by the court's decision concerning the defendant's repayment proposal. You can request a review by a District Judge by asking for an appointment. To do this, complete an Application Notice Form N244, or send a letter, stating why you object to the repayment schedule approved by the court officer (see page 61). You must pay a fee for such an application (usually £65).

The court will then return to you a copy of your Form N244 with details of the place and date of your appointment for you and the defendant to confer informally in the District Judge's 'room' or chambers.

Essentially, the District Judge will ask both you and the defendant questions and then make a decision as to whether the defendant can afford faster repayments or why you cannot show greater patience in receiving your money. The judge, of course, will try to satisfy both you and the defendant in the resolution of the claim.

The judge may advise you then of his decision or decide later. In any event, if the judge decides to change the repayment schedule both you and the defendant will receive notification reflecting the new repayment schedule the defendant is to follow.

It is generally wise to agree to the decision of the court staff as to what is a fair repayment schedule and not seek a review by a District Judge, unless you have information that the defendant has not fully disclosed all of his income.

The court staff are well-experienced on these matters and know what a District Judge is inclined to do. Moreover, a District Judge will not make it a practice to change what has been decided by the court staff. So the odds are small that you will gain much satisfaction by applying for a review by a District Judge.

 ## The defendant admits to owing you, but not the whole amount claimed

If the defendant admits to only part of your claim he will fill in the Form N9B (defence). If he has already paid the amount admitted, he need not fill in Form N9B but otherwise must do so.

This form is sent to the court by the defendant. The court will send you a copy along with a Notice of Part Admission Form N225A.

Form N9A gives you financial information about the defendant's ability to pay that portion of the debt admitted as owing. Form N9B states the defence to that portion of the claim the defendant denies owing.

At this point you may either:

a. accept the defendant's admission of partial liability; or
b. contest the defendant's admission of partial liability and continue to sue for your full claim.

a. Accepting the defendant's part admission

If you decide to accept the defendant's offer of partial payment, then you will want the court to enter 'judgment on acceptance.' Do this by completing parts B and C of Form N225A which is then sent to the court.

Sometimes the defendant proposes to pay the amount offered by immediate payment. But if the defendant is silent on the method of payment then you can request immediate payment.

More often the defendant will propose a repayment schedule. You are now asked to accept a part of your claim in full payment and be paid that amount over an extended time.

If you agree with the defendant's repayment schedule, indicate this on Form N225A. The court will issue a Judgment for Claimant and send copies to you and the defendant to confirm what will be paid, and when.

b. Contesting the defendant's part admission

If you agree with the amount, but disagree with how the defendant proposes to pay it, you should explain on Form N205A why you object to the defendant's offer, what you will accept and how quickly you want it paid.

The process from this point onward is exactly the same as if the defendant agreed to your entire claim but wanted more time to pay it than you are willing to accept.

 ## The defendant denies owing you the money

The defendant may disagree with all of your claim, or you may not be willing to accept the defendant's admission to partial liability.

The defendant will state on Form N9B (defence) why your claim is denied. If the defendant only denies part of your claim (partial admission) the defendant must complete and return to the court both Form N9A (admission) and Form N9B (defence). You will be sent both forms by the court together with Form N225A.

The defendant's defence may be that your claim has already been fully paid and that you are therefore owed nothing. If this defence stated as: 'the amount claimed has been paid' is raised, you will receive from the court a copy of the defendant's Form N9B and Form N236. You must fill in Form N236 and say whether your claim has been fully paid or whether you deny payment and want the case to proceed. Then return the completed Form N236 to the court.

The defendant may say that your claim was partially paid. You should then proceed as stated in the prior section concerning partially admitted claims.

Once a defence is received by the court an Allocation Questionnaire Form N149 is sent to you and the defendant, which must be completed and returned by both parties within 14 days. See completed example beginning on page 55. As the claimant, you must pay a fee when returning the questionnaire, currently £100. If your claim is a money only claim below £1,500 the fee is not payable.

Filling in Allocation Questionnaire
(see completed example on page 57 for reference)

Section A — Settlement
This stay is only automatic where BOTH sides ask for it. Unless you have reason to believe the defendant is asking for it and is genuine in so doing, it is best to put 'No'. The court may order a stay, whether or not all the other parties to the case agree. Where a stay is granted, it will be for an initial period which the judge will specify.

Section B — Location of trial
If you wish the trial to take place at a different court to the one in which the case has proceeded so far, you should say so here. If you began your claim using 'Money Claim Online' (see page 36) the court will already have transferred the claim from the Northampton County Court to the defendant's home court. This is because the court automatically transfers cases to the defendant's home court once he states he is defending the claim. So this is your opportunity to ask the court for trial at a location to suit you. Be realistic though. The court is much more likely to transfer the case to a court that is convenient to both parties and any witnesses.

Section C — Track
If your claim is straightforward, then you should tick the 'yes' box.

Section D — Witnesses
Enter the number of witnesses, not counting yourself, in the box. 'Witnesses' are people who will be coming to court to speak on your behalf. Lawyers call this 'giving evidence'. Include anyone whose evidence you will need to prove your case. If the defendant in his defence admits some aspects of your claim, you do not need to prove them again. Do not include 'experts' (who should be included in the section 'Experts').

Section E — Experts
If in your case someone has done a bad job, then you may need an expert to confirm to the court that this is so. Remember you can only recover a limited amount (the maximum is £200) of the costs of an expert in small claims. So in this section you need to inform the court of any expert evidence you intend using to prove your case. There is a further box asking you to say why you feel you expert needs to attend court to give evidence. One obvious reason why you might need him to come to court is that you have already sent a copy of your expert report to the court, and the defendant has told you he does not accept what your expert has to say in his report. The final box in this section asks you to say if you feel one expert can be used by both you and the defendant. Naturally, if you have spent money proving your claim by asking an expert to give his opinion on the car you bought or the kitchen you had installed, you are unlikely to wish to agree to paying a half-share of another expert's fees. You could suggest your expert could fulfil that role, provided the defendant pays half the bill.

Section F — Hearings
You need to write down the dates when you or your witnesses are not available to give evidence. It is very important to give accurate information here so that you do not have to change a hearing date at the last minute and waste precious time or annoy the court staff. You will need to get in touch with your witnesses promptly and insist that they give you the information you need quickly. This is because you have a limited amount of time in which to complete the Allocation Questionnaire and return it to the court.

There are also boxes to tick to tell the court if you or a witness need an interpreter. If you do, you need to say what kind of interpreter. Obviously, if you or a witness are speech- or hearing-impaired, you may need a sign-language interpreter. Alternatively, you may need a language interpreted.

Section G — Other information
Give any other information that you think is relevant here. If, for instance, there is something special about your case, then say so here. For example:

- If you want to show video/audio evidence.
- If you want the court to make a site visit.

Section H — Fee
The fee is currently £100. If you do not pay it, the court will not fix a hearing date. If you delay returning the Allocation Questionnaire, the court could strike out the claim.

Section H — Signature
You must sign the form or the court will return it to you. If you have a solicitor to represent you then he can do this for you.

Once the court receives both Form N149s, it will be referred to a District Judge for 'allocation'; information in the returned Form N149s will assist him or her. The District Judge can:

a) determine that your case is too complex to be dealt with informally under the Small Claims Track and order an allocation to the Fast or Multi Track;

b) allocate it to the Small Track and:
 i) set a preliminary hearing to consider making special directions; or
 ii) set a small claims hearing.

a. Allocation to Fast or Multi Track

The District Judge's decision to order allocation to the Fast or Multi track can be made when the judge first reviews your file, or after an appointment (conference) or arbitration hearing proves unsuccessful. In the latter instances you will have the opportunity to object.

Transfer to another track will result in a full trial before a Circuit Judge in open court. Such trials are considerably more formal than regular Small Claims Tracks and may require a solicitor if your case is to be represented properly. The cost of a solicitor may alone outweigh any benefits of proceeding in this manner. Furthermore, if you lose in open court you may be ordered to pay for the defendant's solicitor, although the defendant may similarly be liable to pay the costs of your solicitor, if you win.

Considering the £5,000 limit on small claims cases, you should reconsider your case very carefully if reallocation is proposed.

b. A preliminary hearing

The court may hold a preliminary hearing for the consideration of the claim, but only where:

- it considers that special directions are needed to ensure a fair hearing; and it appears necessary for a party to attend at court to ensure that he understands what he must do to comply with the special directions;
- the court is to dispose of the claim as one side has no real prospect of success at a final hearing.

Directions

The court will at this stage give the standard directions which are:

1. Each party shall deliver to every other party and to the court office copies of all documents (including any expert's report) on which he intends to rely at the hearing no later than [   ] [14 days before the hearing.]
2. The original documents shall be brought to the hearing.
3. [Notice of hearing date and time allowed].
4. The court must be informed immediately if the case is settled by agreement before the hearing date.

Special directions

These may be necessary in certain types of case such as:

- road traffic accidents
- building disputes
- landlord and tenant disputes
- holiday and wedding claims

and they may deal with such matters as:

- expert evidence
- exchange of witness statements or documents
- provision of plans and photographs

If you feel there are any reasons why your case should have a preliminary hearing ask for this and give the reasons why in Section G when you return the Allocation Questionnaire.

c. Small Claims hearing

When your claim is allocated to the Small Claims Track the court sends a Notice of Allocation Form N157 (or Form N160 if the claim is above £5,000 and allocated to the Small Claims Track with the defendant's consent), advising you of the date and time of the hearing and what you must do to prepare yourself.

The hearing is held before a District Judge, who listens to each party's case and decides who is right based on the evidence presented. This may include verbal statements, written documents or what an expert tells the court. You will be given guidance on how to prepare and present your case in the next section.

After the hearing, the District Judge will inform you and the defendant of the decision, state who must pay, the amount to be paid and the manner of payment. The judge will also give his reasons for his decision. The court will later write to you confirming the award made.

You and the defendant each have the right to appeal against the District Judge's decision but your appeal will only be successful if you can show that the District Judge applied the law incorrectly or did not conduct the hearing properly. The District Judge's findings of facts cannot be appealed against.

5 The defendant ignores your claim

The defendant must return the Acknowledgement of Service Form to the court stating his intentions within 14 days of the effective date of service. It is not uncommon for the defendant to fail to reply to the claim form within the 14 days. The defendant may feel he is without a defence, or has no assets to lose, or both.

If there is no reply within the time limit then you should ask the court to enter judgment by default. This is done by completing the Request for Judgment and Reply to Admission Form N225. Pay particular attention to how you want the judgment paid. You will naturally want payment at once, but may be more successful in collecting if you grant reasonable instalments. Generally always request payment in full unless you know a good reason not to.

Once Form N225 is completed it should be returned to the court. The court will complete Judgment for Claimant Form N30 advising the defendant of the judgment against him, the amount, how it is to be paid, and where payment shall be made. This is called 'entering a judgment in default'. You will receive from the court a sealed copy of your judgment against the defendant.

The defendant can, however, apply to the court to set aside a judgment entered in default. He must explain why he failed to respond to it and why he disputes it. The court may set aside a judgment if it is satisfied the defendant has a real prospect of successfully defending the claim or if it is satisfied there is some other good reason. If the court agrees to set it aside, the defendant will be allowed to defend the matter and it will then go to a hearing. If this happens you can ask the court to make the setting aside conditional upon the defendant paying the amount in dispute to the court. If this is done, you then have the safety of the money being immediately available if you succeed at the arbitration hearing without the need for taking any enforcement action. However, as already mentioned, obtaining judgment is the easy part. See the section 'Enforcing your judgment' for the steps to enforce the court's decision.

Offers to settle the dispute

Whether you are making or defending a claim, you should always be prepared to consider settling your case. Court cases, however small, are time-consuming. If you receive an offer of settlement, consider it properly even if you decide not to accept the offer. Offers to settle should not be greeted with a 'you cannot be serious' response. Give reasons as to why it is inappropriate or make alternative proposals. If the court decides to hear an application for costs on the grounds of unreasonable behaviour by the claimant or defendant, it is entitled to take rejection of an offer to settle into account. See page 34.

Winning your case

Familiarity with the Small Claims Track does not ensure victory. For that you must know how to:

- win your case;
- enforce your judgment.

In this section you will find the methods that can improve your chances of winning a small claims case whether you are the claimant or the defendant.

Preparing your case

Whether your case will be heard through informal appointment, mediation or open court trial, you must know how to present a winning case. That means preparation.

Assembling the critical facts concerning your dispute, evidence, witnesses, exhibits, documents and other elements needed to prove your case is essential.

Depending on the nature of your complaint you will need the following:

- Written contracts, estimates, proposals or bids.
- Letters and correspondence between you and your adversary.
- Any bills, whether paid or unpaid, as well as cancelled cheques, receipts or other evidence of payment.
- In personal injury cases, medical reports and certification of injury from your doctor as well as medical bills.
- If you could not work due to these injuries, certification of absence from your employer as well as a statement of lost wages.
- If relevant, photographs of injury to yourself or damage to your property.
- In landlord/tenant cases, copies of your lease, rent receipts, security deposits or cleaning fees.
- Witnesses willing to testify for you, or give you a sworn statement of truth.
- If the dispute involves a road accident, a sketch (or photograph) of the accident site.
- A timetable of when important events occurred.

The court may give you 'standard directions for use in claims arising out of road traffic accidents' or 'standard directions for use in claims arising out of building disputes, vehicle repairs and similar contractual claims' after the Allocation stage. These special directions are a good guide to the kind of evidence that will support any claim you make.

Send a copy of your written documents, photographs and sketches to your adversary in advance of the hearing and ask for agreement as to their authenticity and accuracy. This can save time at the hearing and will help avoid any objections at the hearing that can only prolong the proceedings.

When you have assembled these documents, prepare a sequence of facts that includes the following:

- A list of witnesses and the statements each will make.
- A list of documents you will introduce at the hearing.
- A list of statements you will make in presenting your case.

Then reverse your role and anticipate your adversary's case by listing the witnesses, statements, and arguments you believe your adversary will use. With this completed, list the questions you will ask your adversary to disprove his statements. Finally assemble the documents that show your adversary's statements are incorrect.

Remember, you may present three categories of evidence:

1. **Physical evidence** — such as damaged property, as well as documents (contracts, receipts, photographs, etc).
2. **Spoken evidence** — the statements of testimony given by you, or others on your behalf, familiar with certain facts of the case.
3. **Expert evidence** — the testimony of an expert with the professional qualifications to give an opinion on certain facts of the case. Remember you need the permission of the court to call an expert. If you think you will need one, ask for this on Section E of the Allocation Questionnaire.

Presenting your case

Good preparation and presentation are essential to winning your case. If you have prepared your case thoroughly you will greatly improve your chances of success.

Approach the task remembering that using the Small Claims Track is for amateurs. The court does not expect you to act as a professional lawyer.

Even as an amateur you can greatly improve your chances of winning by following these few tips:

1 Practise your presentation

It is a good idea to practise your court presentation at home before family or friends. If they clearly understand your points, it is likely the judge also will.

2 Visit a small claims hearing

Attend a small claims hearing. These are open to the public. Keep in mind that a preliminary hearing and mediation are far less formal and are held in the judge's chambers. You will largely respond to the judge's questions rather than present a court case and cross-examine. When you are familiar with the judge's practices you may change your planned presentation.

3 Act properly

Show up at court punctually. Dress appropriately. Always talk directly to the judge not to your adversary. Address the District Judge as 'Sir' and an open court judge as 'Your Honour'. Most importantly, address your adversary with courtesy. A judge cannot rule in your favour simply because you are well-mannered, but your good demeanour can only reflect well on you. Do not interrupt the judge or your adversary; the judge will always let you answer when he has finished.

4. Be prepared

Write out what you are going to say as a speech and then stick to it. Read it to a friend and ask if it is clear what you are trying to say. Also ask if they have any questions. Then answer those questions.

5. Do not be too legalistic

Present the facts, do not argue the law. You are not a lawyer and the court does not expect a legal discourse. The judge will apply the law to the facts of your case.

Be reasonable. Do not paint a one-sided picture. District Judges are very experienced at seeing both sides and will be more impressed by a party who presents a fair case. If you have a bad point do not ignore it but explain it in the most favourable way you can.

6. Use witnesses properly

If any of the facts of the case are in doubt you must prove what you say is the correct version. Do this either by referring to documents or by another person's testimony. In the case of the latter then generally you must call that person to give evidence to the court.

Always have a signed statement of what that person intends to say. Send it to the other side and ask them to agree that you need not call the witness.

If you need a witness who will not voluntarily come to court a witness summons can be issued by the court. The summons must be issued at least seven days before trial and there is a current fee of £35 if you wish the court to serve it. You will also have to pay the witness's travel and other expenses. If you have several witnesses, ask the most willing and persuasive witness to attend and get written statements from the others.

You may need expert witnesses on technical matters. The Citizens' Advice Bureau may refer you to one. You can also ask the court to allow an independent expert to serve as mediator instead of the District Judge. If you want the court to appoint an expert mediator, then apply to the court for one. If a preliminary appointment has been scheduled, you can request one from the judge at the time of that appointment.

7. Detail your case

Note all the major points you want to make. You will be less likely to forget an item. You will also have dates, amounts, and other important points right at your fingertips.

Remember, if you are the claimant, it is you who has to prove your case to start with. If you do not do this, the defendant will have little work to do in defence. Make it as difficult as you can for the defendant by being fully prepared.

8. Keep your documents in order

Assemble your documents in date order and cross-index for order of presentation (sometimes it helps to put them into a ringbinder file). Also make copies for the judge and your adversary. If you have statements from witnesses, make certain they are signed and dated. If there are more than just a few pages number them in order so that it is easier for the judge to follow. It also makes it much quicker for you to answer any questions that may be asked.

Do not rush. There is no need to worry about time. Once you are in court relax and talk slowly. When your adversary is talking make notes of those points that you will need to refer to and wait until he has finished before replying to them.

9. Recording the hearing

All small claims hearings can be tape recorded by the court, but you may not record them yourself. If you think you may need this facility ask for it before or at the beginning of the hearing.

The judge may direct that all or any part of the proceedings will be tape recorded by the court. A party may obtain a transcript of such a recording on payment of the proper transcriber's charges.

The judge will make a note of the central points of the oral evidence unless it is tape recorded by the court.

A party is entitled to a copy of any note made by the judge.

10. Who says what when?

Small claims hearings usually take place in the District Judge's room, called 'chambers'.

Although the hearing is 'informal' it is nonetheless a court hearing in front of a judge and you should follow the guidelines set out below. The hearing is in public and members of the public can attend, although it is unlikely.

The parties sit either side of the judge at a table. The claimant generally sits to the right of the judge.

Who may appear?

A person may present his own case at a hearing, or a lawyer or lay representative may present it for him. A lay representative may only do so if the person he is representing is present at the hearing or if the court gives permission. However, the court is not obliged to give its permission. It is a matter for the discretion of the court. Any of its officers or employees may represent a limited company.

The running order

As the claimant you put your case first to the judge. Do this by first explaining to the judge briefly what the claim is about and what you want from the defendant. Take the judge through any documents you have and then call your witnesses.

Once you have finished with each witness the defendant may cross-examine them.

After this you may again question them if the cross-examination raised any new points or if you need to clarify any earlier points.

The defendant answers your case by putting his version of events and setting out those areas of your case he disagrees with, again referring to any documents. He calls his witnesses in the same way as before. After he has questioned each one, you can cross-examine them. This simply means testing the accuracy of what they say by asking them about anything which contradicts their version of events and supports yours.

Both parties can have a final summing up of their case and the judge will make his decision. The judge will usually do this immediately but may want to consider the matter and decide later. The judge will set out the details of the case and the points to decide and in whose favour they have been decided. The court will keep a written record of the judge's decision which will explain why you won or lost. This will be important if you want to consider appealing.

If you are at all unsure about anything that has happened ask the judge before you leave chambers.

The running order can vary though. Some District Judges adopt a different sequence. For example, some judges hear all the evidence from all the witnesses and then allow both sides to cross-examine each other and the witnesses. The judge will ask his own questions. As long as you are well prepared, this need not worry you. Remember, District Judges will understand that you are unfamiliar with the court.

How to start proceedings online

This is the alternative to dealing with paper, if you wish to start your claim, or respond to an electronically produced claim against you made online. To do this visit www.hmcourtservice.gov.uk and follow the links to 'Money Claim Online' or go straight to www.moneyclaim.gov.uk. Click on 'User Guide' to find out how to make your claim online. The court fees are collected from you electronically by debit or credit card. All the claims are begun in the name of the Northampton County Court but are produced at the County Court Bulk Centre (CCBC). The fees of the CCBC are modestly reduced to take account of the efficiencies of a bulk system as follows:

- Up to £300 - £20
- UP to £500 - £40
- Up to £1000 - £70
- UP to £5000 - £110

When the CCBC issues a claim form it serves a printed version of the claim form on the defendant by post. A Notice of Issue is sent to the claimant by post. The claim form is deemed to be served on the defendant the fifth day after the claim was issued. You can view an electronic record of the progress of your claim. If the defendant ignores your claim, you can electronically request the court to enter judgment in default. If the defendant accepts your claim you can electronically request entry of judgment on his admission. The defendant can respond to the claim online. Security of the system is assured by the issue of unique customer identification numbers or a password. If you are claiming exemption or remission form court fees you cannot use Money Claim Online.

If you start your claim online and the defendant decides to defend himself the claim will be transferred from the Northampton County Court. If the defendant is an individual, the claim will be transferred to the court nearest the defendant's home court. If the defendant is a business, then the claim will be transferred to your home court. However, this is not necessarily the court in which the trial will take place, as the N149 Allocation questionaire may show it is better for the trial to take place at another court.

Enforcing your judgment

Obtaining a judgment may be considerably easier than getting paid. In some cases a debtor will have few, if any, assets from which to satisfy a judgment. In others, the debtor will simply refuse to pay leaving it to you to enforce judgment.

There are several ways to enforce your small claims judgment. It is important to remember that attempts to enforce judgment are impractical unless you are confident the debtor can pay the debt.

It is wise to check whether there are other outstanding judgments against the debtor. All unpaid judgments are automatically registered at the Registry of County Court Judgments (tel: 020 7380 0133). This service is not available online. For a nominal fee (currently £4.50 per name and address), they will tell you whether the debtor has other unsatisfied judgments. Obviously, if there are many outstanding judgments against the debtor, your chances of getting paid are slight.

Your tactics on enforcement depend on your debtor's situation. Is he employed? Does he have a building society or bank account? Above all, is it likely that he will be able to pay? The method to choose for enforcement will depend on your answers to these questions.

It is always best to encourage voluntary payment from the debtor. You may do this directly with the debtor or ask the court to make an instalment order. The debtor may also ask for an instalment order, and you may inquire about the debtor's assets to determine ability to pay.

What are the methods for enforcing payment on a judgment? There are four:

1. Warrant of execution
2. Attachment of earnings
3. Third party debt order (formerly called a garnishee order)
4. Charging order

All of these methods may be carried out by Money Claim Online www.moneyclaim.gov.uk.

 ## Warrant of execution

A warrant of execution is a request that the County court bailiffs seize any personal belongings of the debtor. Any such belongings are sold and the proceeds of sale after costs will be paid to you up to the value of your judgment.

This method is not usually very effective unless you know that the debtor has assets of value and can direct the bailiffs to them by providing addresses. Bailiffs are only able to act on information you supply to them and do not carry out any investigations themselves. Personal items, such as clothes and tools of the debtor's trade, cannot be seized.

If there are insufficient assets the bailiff will notify the court and you will be advised.

Frequently, the debtor facing a warrant will apply to the court to suspend the warrant and allow him further time to pay the judgment. If the District Judge should suspend the warrant, you may ask to have it reinstated if the debtor does not pay.

A warrant remains in force for one year, but you may renew it continuously upon application to the court.

To issue a warrant of execution send the following to the court:

- A copy of your judgment
- A completed Request for Warrant of Execution Form N323 (see page 60 for an example)
- The appropriate fee, which is:
    - to recoup a payment of less than £125: £35 (CCBC £25)
    - to recoup a payment of more than £125: £55 (CCBC £45)

Attachment of earnings

A more direct way to collect is to have the court order the debtor's employer to make deductions from his earnings and send these payments directly to you. You can attach wages, commissions, and bonuses. You cannot attach Social Security, old age pensions or disability pensions. Servicemen's pay can only be attached through the Defence Council. You can attach wages of an owner of a limited company, but not that of a self-employed debtor, such as a proprietor or partner in a firm.

This method of enforcing will usually only result in payment if the debtor is in secure employment. If he moves job then you have to make a fresh application in respect of any new employment the debtor goes on to.

You can apply for an earnings attachment to the court for the district in which the debtor resides using the Request for Attachment of Earnings Order Form N337. The fee for the court to enforce it is £65. If this is not the court that issued the judgment, you must ask the judgment court to transfer the case to the County court in the debtor's locality.

The application is served on the debtor by the court. Within eight days of its receipt the debtor must complete and return to the court a form detailing his financial information. The court will then issue a provisional order stating the amount to be deducted from the debtor's earnings for each pay period. If you object, you may request a hearing before a Court Officer and present your reasons for a higher amount in person.

Once a final attachment order is entered the employer must obey it or face sanctions from the court. Where there is more than one creditor with an attachment on earnings, the earliest attachment is paid first.

Third party debt order (formerly a garnishee)

A third party debt order (TPDO) is an order directed to a third party who holds money on behalf of, or owes money to, the debtor. It orders the third party to hold any such moneys until there is a hearing at the court to establish if the moneys should be paid to you. You may find that there are other people claiming money from the debtor who also wish to have the money.

Who can you obtain a TPDO against?

- **Banks and building Societies.**
  Only where an account is in the sole name of the debtor.
- **Solicitors.**
  They often hold money on behalf of their clients.
- **Tenants who pay rent to the debtor.**
- **Employers.**
  Only where money is actually due, not where it is merely accruing (see 'Attachment of earnings'). It would be more appropriate to use a TPDO where you expect a single week's or month's pay to cover the debt.

But, each TPDO only works once. It operates at the precise moment it is served on the third party; so that if at that moment the third party does not owe the debtor money, you will be unsuccessful.

Also, the TPDO can pay out any moneys which have a prior call, i.e. if you third party a bank and the debtor has written out a cheque to someone the day before you serve your third party and it is in the clearing system, it will be paid despite your order.

Lastly remember that a TPDO will only be effective if you maintain the element of surprise. Do not give any warning to the debtor that you intend to seek a TPDO or he may simply remove the funds.

To apply for a TPDO you must send the court:

- an Application for Third Party Debt Order Form N349 (see page 65 for an example)
- the appropriate fee, currently £55 per third party

The application must state who you are third partying and if it is a bank account, details of that account.

Important: If you only have details of the bank and not of the account, the bank will search its records for any accounts. Whether or not they find one, you will have to pay their costs. Check to see if you have any old cheques written by the debtor. This will show all the relevant details.

If the court grants the application for a TPDO, known as an Interim Third Party Debt Order, the court will set a hearing date at which the judge will decide how any moneys held by the third party are to be dealt with. Any other claims on the moneys will be settled here.

4 Charging order

A charging order is an order that gives you a legal charge over the debtor's title to a property or shares in a company. This means that the debtor cannot sell the property without you being paid. Whilst it will not provide you with actual payment it does provide good security and is probably the most effective method of enforcing a judgment.

Obviously you first have to know whether the debtor owns any property or shares. If you know where he lives you can search the Land Registry to see if he owns the property. The Land Registers are open to the public and such a search costs £2 if you carry out the search online. You should contact any Land Registry (head office tel: 020 7917 8888 or www.landreg.gov.uk).

There is no way of doing a central search for ownership of shares in limited companies. You can, however, search at Companies House to see if the debtor is a director of a company. If he is, he may own shares in it and this can be checked at Companies House (tel: 0870 333 3636 or www.companieshouse.gov.uk).

To apply for a charging order send the court:

- an application notice (Application for Charging Order on Land or Property Form N379 or Application for Charging Order on Securities Form N380) containing the:
  a. name and address of the debtor and any other known creditors;
  b. amount outstanding on the judgment;
  c. identity of the asset to be charged, i.e. the details of the property and title number;
  d. reason for your belief that the debtor owns the asset, i.e. refer to the land registry title (and attach the original office copy of the property title register which may be obtained from the Land Registry);
- the appropriate fee, currently £55

In a similar way to a TPDO, the court will, if it grants the order, list a hearing date to determine the matter more fully. The court firstly grants an *Interim Charging Order* and after the hearing a Final Charging Order.

You can protect your order by entering a 'caution' against the registered title. To do so, contact the Land Registry. It serves to notify other parties that there are possible outstanding claims on the property and so provides protection against the defendant selling the property before the charging order has been made final. Visit www.landregisteronline.gov.uk for further information.

Other useful remedies

Before you decide which method of collection to use, you will want to know as much as possible about the debtor's financial means.

Order to obtain information (formerly called an oral examination)

To assist you the court can compel the debtor to come to court and answer questions under oath concerning his finances and ability to pay the judgment.

Questioning is very often of little use in extracting information that you can act on. Generally if your debtor has the money to pay you he will do so after a few reminders. If he does not, it is likely he will seek to avoid you altogether, in which case he will be unwilling to attend a questioning or if he does will not give you answers that help you. If a debtor fails to attend that appointment, the court may, as a last resort, issue a warrant for the debtor's arrest.

Questioning is most effective as a simple way of notifying the debtor that you mean business and will not simply let the matter rest.

For an order to obtain information of the debtor, you should apply to the court where the debtor resides or conducts business. You must complete an Application for Order that Debtor Attend Court for Questioning Form N316 (see page 63) and return it to the court with your fee, currently £45. The court will issue an order to the debtor requiring his appearance in court for questioning. The court will also notify you of the date.

You may request the debtor bring documents with him to the hearing to provide details about his means, i.e. payslips or accounts if he is self-employed or bank statements.

At the questioning you may directly question the debtor or request the examination be conducted by the Court Officer. Some typical questions include:

a. What assets do you own?
b. Are you owed any money? If so, by whom?
c. Do you have a job? If so, where? What is your pay?
d. Do you have a bank account? If so, where? What is the account number?
e. Do you rent or own your house or flat? If you own, how is the title held? What is the title number if registered? What is the value of the property? What is owed on the mortgage?
f. What other income do you have? Do you own any shares?
g. Does your spouse have a job? Where? On what salary?
h. What other debts do you have? Are there other wage attachments, warrants or TPDOs against you?

These are illustrative. You can ask any reasonable questions to assist you in discovering how to best collect from the debtor. You should always ask if the debtor wishes to prepare a payment plan. If the debtor proposes one acceptable to you, ask the court to enter it as an order. If the proposed plan is not acceptable, you at least have the information you need to decide how and whether to proceed against the debtor.

 ## Enquiry agents

You can instruct a private firm of enquiry agents to find out information about a person or a business.

Enquiry agents have access to information not readily available to the general public and also know where to look. However, success cannot be guaranteed and the cost of employing an agent may not be worthwhile. In the case of companies and businesses there is a lot of information available if you know where to look. The bigger the company the more information will be available.

In the case of limited companies you can search at Companies House and obtain the registered office of the company, a list of its directors and possibly its recent accounts.

Bankruptcy/winding up proceedings

Another option open to you if your judgment remains unpaid is to commence bankruptcy/winding up proceedings. These can be used as a means of exerting pressure on a debtor in the hope the debtor will then pay voluntarily.

There are two types of proceedings that can be used. The terminology is different in the case of limited companies but the effects are the same, whether it is a company, a business or an individual.

a. Statutory demands

A statutory demand is a formal demand for payment and is the first step in bankruptcy proceedings. It must be on the standard form, available from legal stationers and cannot be used in cases where the sum owed is less than £750.

Once served the debtor has three weeks in which to pay. If the debtor fails to do so you are then at liberty to issue bankruptcy proceedings in the appropriate court.

The real benefit of statutory demands, if you can get over the £750 limit, is that they do not have to be issued by the court and so there is no fee involved. You can simply fill out the standard form and serve it. It is an official-looking document and as a result tends to attract more response, particularly in the case of limited companies.

However, be very careful not to claim anything which is not strictly due. If the debtor disputes the demand the debtor must issue proceedings in the County court to have it set aside. If the debtor does so and is successful you may have to pay the costs.

b. Bankruptcy/insolvency proceedings

This involves using court proceedings to have the debtor declared bankrupt. It is rarely an effective means of obtaining payment and has the added drawback that, as well as the court issue fee, you have to lodge a deposit of £500 for the receiver which is rarely recoverable.

It is an action of last resort and should only be considered if you intend to see it through to the bitter end. For information on how to do this, visit www.insolvency service.gov.uk and follow the links from there.

Glossary of useful terms

adjournment — the postponement to a subsequent date of an action pending in a court.

affidavit — *see* **statement of truth**.

Allocation Questionnaire — a form to be sent to the court giving details of the nature of the action, from which the court allocates the case to one of the three tracks.

appeal — the act of taking your claim, once a judgment is made at the lower court, to the next higher court to try to have it overturned, or to have a new decision on it.

application — a request for an interlocutory order.

arbitration — the determination of the dispute by the court, trade association or independent person as a third party.

attachment of earnings order — used after a judgment is received. The creditor can use this to deduct a percentage of the debtor's wages for a certain time period or until the judgment is paid off.

CCBC — County Court Bulk Centre.

charging order — an order over a defendant's property to secure the amount of the judgment.

civil action — a claim for money owed or property damage which proceeds in the civil courts (e.g. any County court). All small claims are civil claims.

Civil Procedure Rules (CPR) — a new code by which the civil courts operate introduced on 26 April 1999, which unified and replaced High and County Court Rules.

claim — a demand that someone owes you money or property.

Claim Form — the first document filed with the court in a Small Claims Track. This document will typically list the claimant and defendant, the reason the claimant is suing, and the amount. The court issues the claim form.

claimant — the person making a claim.

contempt — a proceeding or an order from the judge saying that an individual has not followed the judge's orders. A criminal charge that may have serious consequences, i.e. jail.

creditor — i.e. the claimant. The individual who is owed money by another.

damages — a sum of money awarded by a court for a breach of contract or to remedy or compensate a wrong caused by the other party.

debtor — i.e. the defendant. The individual who owes money to someone else.

defendant — the individual against whom a claim is made.

default judgment — a judgment entered when a defendant fails to answer a summons.

demand letter — a letter sent by a creditor to the debtor requesting payment on the debt.

District Judge — a judge appointed to supervise the interlocutory and post-judgment stages of the case who can also try cases within a certain financial limit.

expert witness — a witness who gives opinion evidence to assist the court to decide on evidence that requires specialist knowledge. For example, an engineer can give evidence on whether a car had a particular type of fault at the time of sale and whether this would or ought to have been known to the seller.

extension of time — the judge may grant additional time to either side so that they have more time to prepare their case or lodge documents.

Fast Track — for cases with a financial range of £5,000 to £15,000. Limited legal costs are recoverable and a final hearing, which should be no more than one day, is to take place within 30 weeks of allocation.

final hearing — the hearing where each side puts the detail of its case and the court makes a decision.

fixed costs — the limited costs that can be obtained on a successful action under the small claims track.

general damages — the part of a compensation award made to compensate for pain and suffering.

injury — how you have been wronged. What it is that has been broken and needs to be fixed. *See also* **damages**.

interlocutory proceedings — the preliminary stages in civil proceedings occurring between the issue of the claim form and the trial, or final hearing.

issuing fee — the amount you have to pay the court in order to start the proceedings. You must pay the fee when you file the lawsuit.

judgment — the decision of the court in a matter before it.

judgment in default — when the court enters judgment without a trial, because the defendant fails to return a response to the claim.

jurisdiction — whether the court has the power or ability to hear a particular dispute. This depends on many things, including the type of dispute, the amount contested, where the dispute arose, and the citizenship of the parties.

liability — whether someone actually owes you money under the law, for their actions or non-actions.

limitation period — the period allowed by statute in which a claim must be begun. It is six years for most cases but only three for personal injury. Time runs from when the cause of action arises, i.e. when a debt becomes due or the date of an accident.

lists — the order of priority of cases awaiting trial with their expected start dates. A case enters the list after certain preliminary matters have been settled.

litigation friend — the person who conducts proceedings on behalf of a child or patient subject to the Mental Health Act 1983. Usually a parent, but can be anyone appointed by the court.

mediation — this is where the parties seek assistance from a mediator to help them agree a settlement. It differs from arbitration in that no decision is made in favour of one party and both sides must agree to it. Some County courts are now operating such schemes which are very cost effective.

Multi Track — all other cases which are not suitable for the Small Claims or Fast Track. Legal costs are recoverable.

negligence — when the actions or failures to act of someone are wrong in the eyes of the law.

order — an order by the judge directing either party to do something.

order to obtain information — a procedure for the defendant to give details of his financial circumstances to an officer of the court after judgment.

Overriding Objective — Rule 1.1 of the new Civil Procedure Rules which says the court is to deal with cases justly and which introduced the concept of proportionality taking into account the amount, importance and complexity of the issues and the financial position of each party.

personal property — any property other than real estate.

pleading — another name for the documents filed with the court setting out the claim or defence.

preliminary hearing — a hearing where the court can give directions beyond the standard ones. Only used where special circumstances arise in the matter.

secured debt — any obligation guaranteed by collateral of either property or personal property.

service of process — the act of delivering the court documents to the other party in the action.

statement of truth — the allegations of the claimant against the defendant and the relief being claimed, i.e. damages. Formerly called an 'affidavit'.

Small Claims Track — a special procedure in the County court which deals exclusively with small civil actions, below £5,000.

statement of case — the allegations of the claimant against the defendant and the entitlement being claimed, i.e. compensation.

statute of limitation — the time period allowed by the government as to the maximum time allowed between the time a debtor fails to pay you money and the time you sue the debtor. Three years with personal injuries, six years with contracts and property damage.

third party debt order (TPDO) — the act of taking money held for a debtor toward payment of a judgment, i.e. from bank or building society accounts.

tort — a civil wrong or injury.

track — all cases are now allocated to one of the three tracks: Small Claims, Fast and Multi.

trial — a more formal hearing than the final hearing in a Small Claims Track matter. You will be expected to have your witnesses, testimony and other evidence in order for this court appearance.

unsecured debt — an obligation not guaranteed by any form of collateral.

witness summons — a summons requiring a witness to attend court to give evidence or produce a document. Failure to do so is contempt of court.

warrant of execution — a method of requesting the court bailiff to enforce judgment. by seizing the debtor's goods.

Completed example of Claim Form N1

(Continued on next page)

Completed example of Claim Form N1 (continued)

Claim No.

Does, or will, your claim include any issues under the Human Rights Act 1998? ☐ Yes ☑ No

Particulars of Claim (attached)(to follow)

THE CLAIMANT CLAIMS THE SUM OF £500.00 BEING DUE BY THE DEFENDANT UNDER AN INVOICE DATED THE 25 NOVEMBER 2005 NUMBER 5578 FOR GOODS SUPPLIED TO THE DEFENDANT AT HIS REQUEST BY THE CLAIMANT WHICH SUM REMAINS UNPAID.

THE CLAIMANT ALSO CLAIMS INTEREST IN ACCORDANCE WITH S.69 OF THE COUNTY COURTS ACT 1984 AT THE RATE OF 8% PER ANNUM FROM 25/11/05 TO THE DATE HEREOF BEING £9.97 AND CONTINUING AT THE DAILY RATE OF £0.11 UNTIL JUDGMENT OR SOONER PAYMENT.

Statement of Truth

*(I believe)(The Claimant believes) that the facts stated in these particulars of claim are true.
* I am duly authorised by the claimant to sign this statement

Full name JOHN SMITH

Name of claimant's solicitor's firm

signed *John Smith* position or office held
*(Claimant)(Litigation friend)(Claimant's solicitor) (if signing on behalf of firm or company)
*delete as appropriate

Claimant's or claimant's solicitor's address to which documents or payments should be sent if different from overleaf including (if appropriate) details of DX, fax or e-mail.

Example Notes for Claimant Form N1A

Notes for claimant on completing a claim form
Before you begin completing the claim form
- You must think about whether alternative dispute resolution (ADR) is a better way to reach an agreement before going to court. The leaflet 'Making a claim? - Some questions to ask yourself' explains more about ADR and how you can attempt to settle your claim.
- Please read all of these guidance notes. The notes follow the order in which information is required on the form.
- If you are filling in the claim form by hand, please use black ink and write in block capitals.
- Copy the completed claim form and the defendant's notes for guidance so that you have one copy for yourself, one copy for the court and one copy for each defendant. Send or take the forms to the court office with the appropriate fee. The court will tell you how much this is.
- Court staff can help you fill in the claim form and give information about procedure once it has been issued. But they cannot give legal advice. If you need legal advice, for example, about the likely success of your claim or the evidence you need to prove it, you should contact a solicitor or a Citizens Advice Bureau.

Further information may be obtained from the court in a series of free leaflets.

Notes on completing the claim form

Heading
You must fill in the heading of the form to indicate the name of the court where you want the claim to be issued.

The claimant and defendant
As the person issuing the claim, you are called the 'claimant'; the person you are suing is called the 'defendant'. Claimants who are under 18 years old (unless otherwise permitted by the court) and patients within the meaning of the Mental Health Act 1983, must have a litigation friend to issue and conduct court proceedings on their behalf. Court staff will tell you more about what you need to do if this applies to you.

Providing information about yourself and the defendant

full address including postcode
You should provide the full address including postcode for yourself and the defendant. The postcode for any address in the United Kingdom may be obtained free from the Royal Mail Address Management Guide, or their website at www.royalmail.com.

If an address does not have a postcode you will need to ask the judge for permission to serve the claim with this information missing. There is no additional fee for this, but if you omit a postcode and fail to ask permission of the judge the court will not allow your claim to be served on the defendant until you supply the missing postcode or a judge permits service without it.

You must provide the following information about yourself and the defendant according to the capacity in which you are suing and in which the defendant is being sued.

When suing or being sued as:-

an individual:
You must enter his or her full unabbreviated name where known, including their first name and any middle name, their last name and the title by which she or he is known (i.e. Mr., Mrs., Ms., Dr., etc.) and residential address (including postcode and telephone number). Where the defendant is a proprietor of a business, a partner in a firm or an individual sued in the name of a club or other unincorporated association, the address for service should be the usual or last known place of residence or principal place of business of the company, firm or club or other unincorporated association.

Where the individual is:

trading under another name
you must enter his or her full unabbreviated name where known, and the title by which he or she is known and the full name under which he or she is trading, e.g. 'Mr. John Smith trading as Smith's Groceries'.

suing or being sued in a representative capacity
you must say what that capacity is e.g. 'Mr Joe Bloggs as the representative of Mrs Sharon Bloggs (deceased)'.

suing or being sued in the name of a club or other unincorporated association
add the words 'suing/sued on behalf of' followed by the name of the club or other unincorporated association.

an unincorporated business - a firm
In the case of a partnership (other than a limited liability partnership) you must enter the full name of the business followed by the suffix 'a firm'.

Enter the name of the firm followed by the words 'a firm' e.g. 'Bandbox - a firm' and an address including postcode for service. This may either be one of the partners residential addresses or the principal or last known place of business of the firm.

N1A Notes for claimant (04.06) HMCS

(Continued on next page)

Example Notes for Claimant Form N1A (continued)

a company registered in England and Wales or a Limited Liability Partnership

In the case of a registered company or limited liability partnership, you must enter the full name of the company or partnership followed by the appropriate suffix, i.e. Ltd, Plc, LLP. You must provide an address, including postcode which is either the company's registered office or any place of business in England and Wales that has a real, or the most, connection with the claim e.g. a shop where goods were bought.

a corporation (other than a company)
enter the full name of the corporation and any suffix if appropriate and the address including postcode in England and Wales which is either its principal office or any other place where the corporation carries on activities and which has a real connection with the claim.

an overseas company (defined by s744 of the Companies Act 1985)
You must enter the company's full name and any suffix if appropriate and address including postcode. The address must either be the registered address under s691 of the Act or the address of the place of business having a real, or the most, connection with the claim.

under 18 write '(a child by Mr Joe Bloggs his litigation friend)' after the name. If the child is conducting proceedings on their own behalf write '(a child)' after the child's name.

a patient within the meaning of the Mental Health Act 1983 write '(by Mr Joe Bloggs his litigation friend)' after the patient's name.

Brief details of claim
You must set out under **this** heading:
- a concise statement of the nature of your claim
- the remedy you are seeking e.g. payment of money;

Value
If you are claiming a **fixed amount of money** (a 'specified amount') write the amount in the box at the bottom right-hand corner of the claim form against 'amount claimed'.

If you are <u>not</u> claiming a fixed amount of money (an 'unspecified amount') under 'Value' write "I expect to recover" followed by whichever of the following applies to your claim:
- 'not more than £5,000' **or**
- 'more than £5,000 but not more than £15,000' **or**
- 'more than £15,000'

If you are **not able** to put a value on your claim, write 'I cannot say how much I expect to recover'.

Personal injuries
If your claim is for 'not more than £5,000' and includes a claim for personal injuries, you must also write 'My claim includes a claim for personal injuries and the amount I expect to recover as damages for pain, suffering and loss of amenity is' followed by either:
- 'not more than £1,000' **or**
- 'more than £1,000'

Housing disrepair
If your claim is for 'not more than £5,000' and includes a claim for housing disrepair relating to residential premises, you must also write 'My claim includes a claim against my landlord for housing disrepair relating to residential premises. The cost of the repairs or other work is estimated to be' followed by either:
- 'not more than £1,000' **or**
- 'more than £1,000'

If within this claim, you are making a claim for other damages, you must also write:

'I expect to recover as damages' followed by either:
- 'not more than £1,000' **or**
- 'more than £1,000'

Defendant's name and address
Enter in this box the title, full names, address and postcode of the defendant receiving the claim form (ie. one claim form for each defendant). If the defendant is to be served outside England and Wales, you may need to obtain the court's permission.

Particulars of claim
You must set out under this heading:
- a concise statement of the facts on which you rely
- a statement (if applicable) to the effect that you are seeking aggravated damages or exemplary damages
- details of any interest which you are claiming
- any other matters required for your type of claim as set out in the relevant practice direction

Statement of truth
This must be signed by you, or by your solicitor or your litigation friend, if appropriate.

Where the claimant is a registered company or a corporation the claim must be signed by either the director, treasurer, secretary, chief executive, manager or other officer of the company or (in the case of a corporation) the mayor, chairman, president or town clerk.

Address for documents
Insert in this box the address at which you wish to receive documents and/or payments, if different from the address you have already given under the heading 'Claimant'. The address must be in England or Wales. If you are willing to accept service by DX, fax or e-mail, add details.

Completed example of Certificate of Service Form N215

Certificate of service

Name of court	Claim No.
CENTRAL LONDON COUNTY COURT	CL4 12345

Name of Claimant: JOHN SMITH

Name of Defendant: JAMES SHERBERT

On the **28 FEBRUARY 2006** ...(insert date)

the **CLAIM FORM** ...(insert title or description of documents served)

a copy of which is attached to this notice was served on (insert name of person served, including position i.e. partner, director if appropriate)

JAMES SHERBERT

Tick as appropriate

- [ ] by first class post or (with effect from 6th April 2006) an alternative service which provides for delivery on the next working day.
- [ ] by Document Exchange
- [✔] by delivering to or leaving at a permitted place (see notes overleaf)
- [ ] by personally handing it to or leaving it with (please specify)
- [ ] by fax machine (..........time sent) (you may want to enclose a copy of the transmission sheet)
- [ ] by other electronic means (please specify)
- [ ] by other means permitted by the court (please specify)

at (insert address where service effected, include fax or DX number, e-mail address or other electronic identification)

14 SKINNER HOUSE
WALTHAM ROAD
LONDON SE2 7BX

being the [ ] claimant's [✔] defendant's [ ] solicitor's [ ] litigation friend:

- [✔] usual residence
- [ ] last known residence
- [ ] place of business
- [ ] principal place of business
- [ ] last known place of business
- [ ] principal office of the corporation
- [ ] principal office of the company
- [ ] other (please specify)

The date of service is therefore deemed to be **28 FEBRUARY 2006** (insert date - see overleaf for guidance)

I believe that the facts stated in this Certificate are true.

Full name: JOHN RYAN SMITH

Signed: *John Smith*
(Claimant)~~(Defendant)(Claimant's solicitor)~~

Position or office held:
(if signing on behalf of firm or company)

Date: 28 FEB 2006

N215 Certificate of service (01.06) © Crown copyright. Published by Lawpack Publishing Limited.

(Continued on next page)

Completed example of Certificate of Service Form N215 (continued)

Notes for guidance
Please note that these notes are only a guide and are not exhaustive
If you are in doubt you should refer to Part 6 of the rules

Where to serve

Nature of party to be served	Permitted place of service
Individual	• Usual or last known residence
Proprietor of business	• Usual or last known residence; or • Place of business or last known place of business
Individual who is suing or being sued in the name of a firm	• Usual or last known residence; or • Principal or last known place of business of the firm
Corporation (incorporated in England and Wales) other than a company	• Principal office of the corporation; or • any place of within the jurisdiction where the corporation carries on its activities and which has a real connection with the claim
Company registered in England and Wales	• Principal office of the company or corporation; or • any place of business of the company within the jurisdiction which has a real connection with the claim

Personal Service - A document is served personally on an individual by leaving it with that individual. A document is served personally on a company or other corporation by leaving it with a person holding a senior position within the company or corporation. In the case of a partnership, you must leave it with either a partner or a person having control or management at the principal place of business. Where a solicitor is authorised to accept service on behalf of a party, service must be effected on the solicitor, unless otherwise ordered.

Deemed Service - Part 6.7(1). A document which is served in accordance with these rules or any relevant practice direction shall be deemed to be served on the day shown in the following table.

Method of service	Deemed day of service
First class post or (with effect from 6th April 2006) an alternative service which provides for delivery on the next working day.	The second day after it was posted
Document exchange	The second day after it was left at the document exchange
Delivering the document to or leaving it at a permitted address	The day after it was delivered to or left at the permitted address
Fax	If it is transmitted on a business day before 4 p.m., on that day, or otherwise on the business day after the day on which it was transmitted
Other electronic method	The second day after the day on which it was transmitted

- If a document is served personally after 5 p.m. on a business day, or at any time on a Saturday, Sunday or a bank holiday, the document shall, for the purpose of calculating any period of time after service of the document, be treated as having been served on the next business day.

- In this context "business day" means any day except Saturday, Sunday or a bank holiday; and "bank holiday" includes Christmas Day and Good Friday.

Service of documents on children and patients - The rules relating to service on children and patients are contained in Part 6.6 of the rules.

Claim Forms - The general rules about service are subject to the special rules about service of claim forms contained in rules 6.12 to 6.16.

Completed example of Defendant's Reply Form N9A (Admission)

Admission (specified amount)

- You have a limited number of days to complete and return this form
- Before completing this form, please read the notes for guidance attached to the claim form

When to fill in this form
Only fill in this form if:
- you are admitting all of the claim **and** you are asking for time to pay; or
- you are admitting part of the claim. (You should also complete form N9B)

How to fill in this form
- Tick the correct boxes and give as much information as you can. **Then sign and date the form.** If necessary provide details on a separate sheet, add the claim number and attach it to this form.
- Make your offer of payment in box 11 on the back of this form. **If you make no offer the claimant will decide how much and when you should pay.**
- If you are not an individual, you should ensure that you provide sufficient details about the assets and liabilities of your firm, company or corporation to support any offer of payment made in box 11.
- You can get help to complete this form at **any** county court office or Citizens Advice Bureau.

Where to send this form
- **If you admit the claim in full**
Send the completed form to the address shown on the claim form as one to which documents should be sent.
- **If you admit only part of the claim**
Send the form **to the court** at the address given on the claim form, together with the defence form (N9B).

How much of the claim do you admit?
- [✓] I admit the full amount claimed as shown on the claim form **or**
- [ ] I admit the amount of £ _____

Name of court	CENTRAL LONDON COUNTY COURT
Claim No.	CL4 12345
Claimant (including ref.)	JOHN SMITH (JS/as)
Defendant	JAME SHERBERT

1 Personal details

Surname	SHERBERT
Forename	JAMES

[✓] Mr   [ ] Mrs   [ ] Miss   [ ] Ms
[✓] Married   [ ] Single   [ ] Other (specify)

Date of birth: 0 5 0 9 1 9 6 6

Address:
14 SKINNER HOUSE
WALTHAM ROAD
LONDON

Postcode: SE2 7BX

Tel. no. 020 7123 4567

2 Dependants (people you look after financially)

Number of children in each age group
- under 11: 2
- 11-15:
- 16-17:
- 18 & over:

Other dependants (give details): WIFE

3 Employment

[ ] I am employed as a _____
My employer is _____
Jobs other than main job (give details) _____

[✓] I am self employed as a ELECTRICIAN
Annual turnover is.......... £ 16,000

[ ] I am **not** in arrears with my national insurance contributions, income tax and VAT

[ ] I am in arrears and I owe.......... £ _____

Give details of:
(a) contracts and other work in hand: VARIES FROM WEEK TO WEEK
(b) any sums due for work done: NONE

[ ] I have been unemployed for ___ years ___ months

[ ] I am a pensioner

4 Bank account and savings

[✓] I have a bank account
 - [✓] The account is in credit by........ £ 350.00
 - [ ] The account is overdrawn by.... £ _____

[ ] I have a savings or building society account
 - The amount in the account is.......... £ _____

5 Residence

I live in:
- [ ] my own house
- [ ] my jointly owned house
- [ ] rented accommodation
- [ ] lodgings
- [✓] council accommodation

N9A Form of admission (specified amount) (04.06)   HMCS

(Continued on next page)

Completed example of Defendant's Reply Form N9A (Admission)
(continued)

6 Income

My usual take home pay *(including overtime, commission, bonuses etc)*	£ 220	per WK
Income support	£	per
Child benefit(s)	£	per
Other state benefit(s)	£	per
My pension(s)	£	per
Others living in my home give me	£	per
Other income *(give details below)*		
	£	per
	£	per
	£	per
Total income	**£ 220**	**per WK**

7 Expenses
(Do not include any payments made by other members of the household out of their own income)

I have regular expenses as follows:

Mortgage *(including second mortgage)*	£ –	per
Rent	£ 25	per WK
Council tax	£ 6	per WK
Gas	£ 3	per WK
Electricity	£ 5	per WK
Water charges	£ 2	per WK
TV rental and licence	£ 15	per WK
HP repayments	£ 28	per WK
Mail order	£ –	per
Housekeeping, food, school meals	£ 75	per WK
Travelling expenses	£ 15	per WK
Children's clothing	£ 5	per WK
Maintenance payments	£ –	per
Others *(not court orders or credit debts listed in boxes 9 and 10)*		
	£ –	per
	£ –	per
	£ –	per
Total expenses	**£ 179**	**per WK**

8 Priority debts *(This section is for arrears only. Do not include regular expenses listed in box 7.)*

Rent arrears	£	per
Mortgage arrears	£	per
Council tax/Community Charge arrears	£	per
Water charges arrears	£	per
Fuel debts: Gas	£	per
Electricity	£	per
Other	£	per
Maintenance arrears	£	per
Others *(give details below)*		
	£	per
	£	per
Total priority debts	**£**	**per**

9 Court orders

Court	Claim No.	£	per
N/A			

Total court order instalments £ per

Of the payments above, I am behind with payments to *(please list)*

10 Credit debts

Loans and credit card debts *(please list)*

N/A	£	per
	£	per
	£	per

Of the payments above, I am behind with payments to *(please list)*

11 Offer of payment

☐ I can pay the amount admitted on ☐
or
☑ I can pay by monthly instalments of £

If you cannot pay immediately, please give brief reasons below

12 Declaration   I declare that the details I have given above are true to the best of my knowledge

Signed	James Sherbert	Position or office held *(if signing on behalf of firm or company)*	N/A
Date	12/03/06		

Completed example of Defendant's Reply Form N9B (Defence)

Defence and Counterclaim (specified amount)

- Fill in this form if you wish to dispute all or part of the claim and/or make a claim against the claimant (counterclaim).
- You have a limited number of days to complete and return this form to the court.
- Before completing this form, please read the notes for guidance attached to the claim form.
- Please ensure that all boxes at the top right of this form are completed. You can obtain the correct names and number from the claim form. The court cannot trace your case without this information.

How to fill in this form
- Complete sections 1 and 2. Tick the correct boxes and give the other details asked for.
- Set out your defence in section 3. If necessary continue on a separate piece of paper making sure that the claim number is clearly shown on it. In your defence you must state which allegations in the particulars of claim you deny and your reasons for doing so. **If you fail to deny an allegation it may be taken that you admit it.**
- If you dispute only some of the allegations you must
  - specify which you admit and which you deny; and
  - give your own version of events if different from the claimant's.

Name of court	CENTRAL LONDON COUNTY COURT
Claim No.	CL4 12345
Claimant (including ref.)	JOHN SMITH (JS/as)
Defendant	JAMES SHERBERT

- If you wish to make a claim against the claimant (a counterclaim) complete section 4.
- Complete and sign section 5 before sending this form to the court. Keep a copy of the claim form and this form.

Community Legal Service Fund (CLSF)
You may qualify for assistance from the CLSF (this used to be called 'legal aid') to meet some or all of your legal costs. Ask about the CLSF at any county court office or any information or help point which displays this logo.

1. How much of the claim do you dispute?
- ☐ I dispute the full amount claimed as shown on the claim form
  or
- ☐ I admit the amount of £ _____

If you dispute only part of the claim you must **either**:
- pay the amount admitted to the person named at the address for payment on the claim form (see How to Pay in the notes on the back of, or attached to, the claim form). Then send this defence to the court
  or
- complete the admission form **and** this defence form and send them to the court.

  ☐ I paid the amount admitted on (*date*) _____
  or
  ☑ I enclose the completed form of admission
  (*go to section 2*)

2. Do you dispute this claim because you have already paid it? *Tick whichever applies*

☑ No (*go to section 3*)

☐ Yes I paid £ _____ to the claimant
on _____ (*before the claim form was issued*)

Give details of where and how you paid it in the box below (*then go to section 5*)

3. Defence

N9B Defence and Counterclaim (specified amount)(04.06) HMCS

(Continued on next page)

Completed example of Defendant's Reply Form N9B (Defence) (continued)

Defence (continued)   Claim No.

4. If you wish to make a claim against the claimant (a counterclaim)

If your claim is for a specific sum of money, how much are you claiming? £ N/A

I enclose the counterclaim fee of £

- To start your counterclaim, you will have to pay a fee. Court staff can tell you how much you have to pay.
- You may not be able to make a counterclaim where the claimant is the Crown (e.g. a Government Department). Ask at your local county court office for further information.

My claim is for *(please specify nature of claim)*

What are your reasons for making the counterclaim?
If you need to continue on a separate sheet put the claim number in the top right hand corner

N/A

5. Signed
(To be signed by you or by your solicitor or litigation friend)

*(I believe)(~~The defendant believes~~) that the facts stated in this form are true. ~~I am duly authorised by the defendant to sign this statement~~

James Sherbert

delete as appropriate

Position or office held (if signing on behalf of firm or company)   N/A

Defendant's date of birth, if an individual   0 5 0 9 1 9 6 6

Date   12/03/06

Give an address to which notices about this case can be sent to you

14 SKINNER HOUSE
WALTHAM ROAD
LONDON

Postcode SE2 7BX

Tel. no. 020 7123 4567

if applicable

fax no.

DX no.

e-mail

Completed example of Request for Judgment and Reply to Admission Form N225

Request for judgment and reply to admission (specified amount)

- Tick box A or B. If you tick box B you must complete the details in that part and in part D. Make sure that all the case details are given. Remember to sign and date the form. Your signature certifies that the information you have given is correct.
- If the defendant has given an address on the form of admission to which correspondence should be sent, which is different from the address shown on the claim form, you must tell the court.
- Return the completed form to the court.

In the CENTRAL LONDON COUNTY COURT

Claim No. CL4 12345

Claimant (including ref)

Defendant (including ref) JAMES SHERBERT JS/as

A ☐ The defendant has not filed an admission or defence to my claim

Complete all the judgment details at D. Decide how and when you want the defendant to pay. You can ask for the judgment to be paid by instalments or in one payment.

B ☑ The defendant admits that all the money is owed

Tick only **one** box below and complete all the judgment details at D.

☑ I accept the defendant's proposal for payment

Say how the defendant intends to pay. The court will send the defendant an order to pay. You will also be sent a copy.

☐ The defendant has not made any proposal for payment

Say how you want the defendant to pay. You can ask for the judgment to be paid by instalments or in one payment. The court will send the defendant an order to pay. You will also be sent a copy.

☐ I do NOT accept the defendant's proposal for payment

Say how you want the defendant to pay. Give your reasons for objecting to the defendant's offer of payment in the space opposite. (Continue on the back of this form if necessary.) Send this form to the court **with defendant's admission N9A**. The court will fix a rate of payment and send the defendant an order to pay. You will also be sent a copy.

C

☑ Defendant's date of birth is not stated in the form of reply but is known to the claimant as

`0 5 0 9 1 9 6 6`

☐ Defendant's date of birth is not stated in the form of reply and is not known to the claimant.

D Judgment details

I would like the judgment to be paid

☑ (immediately)

☐ (by instalments of £ _____ per month)

☐ (in full by _____)

Amount of claim as admitted	300	00
(including interest at date of issue)		
Interest since date of claim (if any)		
Period from 25/11/05 to 22/03/06		
Rate 8 %		
Court fees shown on claim	80	00
Solicitor's costs (if any) on issuing claim		
Sub Total	600	53
Solicitor's costs (if any) on entering judgment		
Sub Total	600	53
Deduct amount (if any) paid since issue		
Amount payable by defendant	600	53

I certify that the information given is correct

Signed *John Smith*
(Claimant)(~~Litigation friend or claimant's solicitor~~)

Position or office held _____
(if signing on behalf of firm or company)

Date 22/03/06

The court office at _____ is open between 10 am and 4 pm Monday to Friday. When corresponding with the court, please address forms and letters to the Court Manager and quote the Claim number.

N225 Request for judgment and reply to admission (specified amount) (04.06)   © Crown copyright. Published by Lawpack Publishing Limited.

Completed example of Allocation Questionnaire Form N149

Allocation questionnaire
(Small claims track)

In the CENTRAL LONDON COUNTY COURT County Court

Claim No. CL4 12345

Last date for filing with court office

Completed by, or on behalf of, (print name)

JOHN SMITH

who is the [Claimant][~~Defendant~~] in this claim.

> **Please read the notes on page 4 before completing the questionnaire.**
>
> You must complete this questionnaire. It will be used to assist the court in the management of the claim.
>
> You should note the date by which it must be returned and the name of the court it should be returned to since this may be different from the court where proceedings were issued. This information is shown on the Form N152 which came with this questionnaire.
>
> If you have settled this claim (or if you settle it on a future date) and therefore do not need a hearing, you must let the court know immediately.

A Settlement

Do you wish any further action in this claim to be postponed for one month so that you and the other party can attempt to settle the claim either by informal discussion or by alternative dispute resolution? ☑ Yes ☐ No

B Location of hearing

The claim will be heard in the court to which this form must be returned. Is there any reason why it should be transferred to another court to be heard? ☐ Yes ☑ No

If Yes, say which court and why

C Track

Do you agree that the small claims track is the most suitable track for this claim? ☑ Yes ☐ No

If No, please say why

N149 Allocation questionnaire (Small claims tracks) (11.05) HMCS

(Continued on next page)

Completed example of Allocation Questionnaire Form N149 (continued)

D Witnesses

So far as you know at this stage, how many witnesses (other than yourself) do you intend to call to give evidence at the hearing?

E Experts

Do you want permission to use an expert's report at the hearing? *(see notes)* ☐ Yes ☑ No

If Yes, what will the expert's evidence deal with?

Have you already obtained an expert's report? ☐ Yes ☑ No

If Yes, have you given a copy of that report to the other party? ☐ Yes ☑ No

In addition to using an expert's report do you want your expert to attend the hearing and give evidence? ☐ Yes ☑ No

If Yes, give the reasons why you think their attendance is necessary:

The court may order the appointment of a single expert who can be instructed by both parties. If you think this would not be appropriate, please say why.

F Hearing

Are there any days within the next four months when you, an expert or a witness will not be able to attend court for the hearing? ☐ Yes ☑ No

If Yes, please give details

	Dates not available
Yourself	
Expert	
Other essential witness	

Will you be using an interpreter at the hearing either for yourself or for a witness? *(see notes)* ☐ Yes ☑ No

If Yes, please specify the type of interpreter

2

(Continued on next page)

Completed example of Allocation Questionnaire Form N149 (continued)

G Other information

In the space below, set out any other information you consider will help the judge to manage or clarify the claim, including any other information you consider should be supplied by the other party.

H Fee

Have you attached the fee for filing this allocation questionnaire? ☑ Yes   ☐ No

I Signature *(see notes)*

Signed: *John Smith*   Date: 5th April 2006

Print full name

If a solicitor is acting for you please enter the firm's name, reference number and full postal address including (if appropriate) details of fax number, e-mail address, Document Exchange (DX) number. Otherwise, please enter your details as appropriate. This will assist the court in contacting you, if necessary at short notice.

Ref. no.	
Telephone no.	
Mobile no.	
Fax no.	
e-mail address	
DX no.	

(Continued on next page)

Completed example of Allocation Questionnaire Form N149 (continued)

Notes for completing a small claims track allocation questionnaire

- If the claim is not settled, a judge must allocate it to an appropriate case management track and if necessary give directions for the conduct of the case. The most just and cost-effective track for this claim appears to be the small claims track and you must now complete the attached questionnaire to help the judge decide.
- If you fail to return the allocation questionnaire by the date given, the judge may make an order that leads to your claim or defence being 'struck out' (Rule 3.4): this means you could not proceed with it. Alternatively the judge may order an allocation hearing at which the judge can order any party who has not filed their questionnaire to pay, immediately, the costs of that hearing.
- The letters below refer to the corresponding sections of the questionnaire and tell you what information is needed, including where appropriate other guidance and references to court rules.

A. Settlement
Even at this stage, you should still think about whether you and the other party can settle your dispute without going to court. If you wish no further action to be taken on the claim for a month (called a 'stay') and tick 'yes' to this question, the court may allow a stay whether or not all the parties to the claim agree. Where a stay is granted, it will be for an initial period of one month (Rule 26.4). You may seek to settle the claim either by informal discussion with the other party or by alternative dispute resolution (ADR). ADR covers a range of different processes which can help settle disputes. More information is available in the Legal Services Commission leaflet 'Alternatives to Court' free from any county court or from the LSC leaflet line 0845 3000 343

B. Location
Automatic transfer to a defendant's local court applies to certain claims (Rule 26.2). This claim will be heard at the court to which you have been asked to return this questionnaire but the court will consider an application for it to be transferred to another court <u>if there is a good reason to do so.</u>

C. Track
The basic guide by which claims are normally allocated to a track is the amount in dispute, although other factors such as the complexity of the case will also be considered (Rules 26.6 - 26.8). A leaflet available from the court office explains the limits in greater detail.

Small Claims track	Disputes valued at not more than £5,000 except
	• those including a claim for personal injuries worth over £1,000 and
	• those for housing disrepair where either the cost of repairs or other work exceeds £1,000 or any other claim for damages exceeds £1,000
Fast track	Disputes valued at more than £5,000 but not more than £15,000
Multi-track	Disputes over £15,000

D. Witnesses
Enter the number of witnesses you intend to call to give evidence **not** including yourself or any expert witness.

E. Experts
You should **not** obtain an expert's report until you receive the court's direction. If you have already obtained a report, please attach it to your completed questionnaire.

F. Hearing
Dates to avoid: You should only enter those dates where you, your expert or an essential witness will not be able to attend court because of a holiday or other commitments.
Interpreters: In some circumstances the court will arrange for, and meet the cost of, an interpreter. If you require an interpreter, you should contact the court immediately. For further details visit the HMCS website www.hmcourts-service.gov.uk under "Information about"

G. Other information
Give details of any other information that you consider will help the judge to manage the claim, referring as necessary to any documents you have attached. Bear in mind however that at this stage you need not attach all other documents which you wish the court to consider at the hearing. This is something you will later be asked to provide.

H. Fee
You should note that if you do not pay this fee it might lead to your claim being struck out (Rule 3.7). If you are the claimant, depending on the value of your claim, you may have to pay a court fee. If you have not applied for fee exemption or remission, the fee must be sent to the court at the same time as your completed questionnaire. Further details can be obtained from the Fees leaflet EX50 available free from any county court or from Her Majesty's Courts Service website www.hmcourts-service.gov.uk

I. Signature
This questionnaire must be signed by only the party to the claim or litigation friend or legal representative.

(Continued on next page)

Completed example of Request for Warrant of Execution Form N323

Request for Warrant of Execution

to be completed and signed by the claimant or his solicitor and sent to the court with the appropriate fee

1 Claimant's name and address

JOHN SMITH
1 THE HIGH STREET
LONDON
W1

In the CENTRAL LONDON **County Court**

Claim Number CL4 12345

2 Name and address for service and payment *(if different from above)*
Ref/Tel No.

N/A

JS/as   020 7234 5678

for court use only
Warrant no.
Issue date:
Warrant applied for at   o'clock
Foreign court code/name:

3 Defendant's name and address

JAMES SHERBERT
14 SKINNER HOUSE
WALTHAM ROAD
LONDON
SE2 7BX

4 Warrant details

(A) Balance due at date of this request	598	33
(B) Amount for which warrant to issue	598	33
Issue fee	50	00
Solicitor's costs		
Land Registry fee		
TOTAL	648	33

If the amount of the warrant at (B) is less than the balance at (A), the sum due after the warrant is paid will be

I certify that the whole or part of any instalments due under the judgment or order have not been paid and the balance now due is as shown

Signed *John Smith*

Claimant (~~Solicitor~~)

Dated 10 MAY 2006

IMPORTANT
You must inform the court immediately of any payments you receive after you have sent this request to the court

You should provide a contact number so that the bailiff can speak to you if he/she needs to:

Daytime phone number: Evening phone number (if possible):
Contact name (where appropriate):
Defendant's phone number (if known):

If you have any other information which may help the bailiff or if you have reason to believe that the bailiff may encounter any difficulties you should write it below.

N323 – Request for warrant of execution (4.99)

Completed example of Application Notice Form N244

Application Notice

In the CENTRAL LONDON

You should provide this information for listing the application

1. How do you wish to have your application dealt with
   a) at a hearing? ☐ ⎫
   b) at a telephone conference? ☐ ⎬ complete all questions below
   c) without a hearing? ☐   complete Qs 5 and 6 below

2. Give a time estimate for the hearing/conference
   _____(hours)_____(mins)

3. Is this agreed by all parties? ☐ Yes ☐ No

4. Give dates of any trial period or fixed trial date _____

5. Level of judge _____

6. Parties to be served _____

Claim no.	CL4 12345
Warrant no. (If applicable)	
Claimant (including ref.)	JOHN SMITH JS/as
Defendant(s) (including ref.)	JAMES SHERBERT
Date	2 JUNE 2006

Note You must complete Parts A and B, and Part C if applicable. Send any relevant fee and the completed application to the court with any draft order, witness statement or other evidence; and sufficient copies for service on each respondent.

Part A

1. Enter your full name, or name of solicitor

   I ~~(We)~~[1] JOHN SMITH ~~(on behalf of)~~ (the claimant) ~~(the defendant)~~

2. State clearly what order you are seeking and if possible attach a draft

   intend to apply for an order (a draft of which is attached) that[2]

   THE COURT REVIEW ITS DECISION REGARDING THE DEFENDANT'S PAYMENTS

   because[3]

3. Briefly set out why you are seeking the order. Include the material facts on which you rely, identifying any rule or statutory provision

   THE DEFENDANT HAS A PART-TIME JOB AS A SECURITY OFFICER WHICH HE DID NOT REVEAL, AND I BELIEVE HE IS THEREFORE ABLE TO PAY THE WHOLE SUM IMMEDIATELY, OR MORE QUICKLY IN LARGER INSTALMENTS

Part B

I ~~(We)~~ wish to rely on: *tick one box*

the attached (witness statement)(affidavit) ☐   my statement of case ☐

evidence in Part C in support of my application ✓

4. If you are not already a party to the proceedings, you must provide an address for service of documents

Signed *John Smith*

(Applicant)~~(‘s Solicitor)~~~~(‘s litigation friend)~~

Position or office held _____

(if signing on behalf of firm or company)

Address to which documents about this claim should be sent (including reference if appropriate)[4]

	if applicable
1 THE HIGH STREET LONDON	fax no.
	DX no.
Tel. no. 020 7123 4567 Postcode W1	e-mail

The court office at

is open from 10am to 4pm Monday to Friday. When corresponding with the court please address forms or letters to the Court Manager and quote the claim number.

N244 Application Notice (4.00)

(Continued on next page)

Completed example of Application Notice Form N244 (continued)

Part C Claim No. CL4 12345

I (~~We~~) wish to rely on the following evidence in support of this application:

LETTER FROM THE DEFENDANT'S EMPLOYER CONFIRMING THAT HE HAS A PART-TIME JOB WITH THEM.

Statement of Truth

*(I believe) *(~~The applicant believes~~) that the facts stated in Part C are true
*delete as appropriate

Signed *John Smith*

(Applicant)(~~'s Solicitor~~)(~~'s litigation friend~~)

Position or office held

(if signing on behalf of firm or company)

Date 02/06/06

Completed example of Application for Order that Debtor Attend Court for Questioning Form N316

Application for order that debtor attend court for questioning

In the CENTRAL LONDON COUNTY COURT

Claim No. CL4 12345

Appn. No.

JOHN SMITH — Claimant

JAMES SHERBERT — Defendant

The [claimant] [defendant] ('the judgment creditor') applies for an order that the [defendant] [claimant] ('the judgment debtor') attend court to provide information about the judgment debtor's means and any other information needed to enforce the judgment or order given on 1 JUNE 20 06 [by the CENTRAL LONDON COUNTY COURT in claim no. CL4 12345].

1. Judgment debtor

The judgment debtor is JAMES SHERBERT

whose address is 14 SKINNER HOUSE, WALTHAM ROAD, LONDON

Postcode SE2 7BX

2. Judgment debt or order

[The judgment or order required the judgment debtor to pay £ 648.33 (including any costs and interest). The amount now owing is £ 648.33 [which includes further interest payable on the judgment debt]].

[The judgment or order required the judgment debtor to

PAY £648.33 FORTHWITH

]

Note:

Questioning and documents

Questioning will be by a court officer unless a judge agrees there are compelling reasons for questioning to take place before a judge. Normally the court officer will ask the questions set out in Form EX140 and the judgment debtor will be told to produce all relevant documents including:

- pay slips
- bank statements
- building society books
- share certificates
- rent book

- mortgage statement
- hire purchase and similar agreements
- court orders
- any other outstanding bills
- electricity, gas, water and council tax bills for the past year.

and in the case of a business

- bills owed to it
- 2 years' accounts
- current management accounts.

Complete sections 3,4 and 5 only if applicable.
The statement of truth overleaf must be completed.

N316 Application for order that debtor attend court for questioning (03.02)

(Continued on next page)

Completed example of Application for Order that Debtor Attend Court for Questioning Form N316 (continued)

3. [Attached is a list of questions which the judgment creditor wishes the court officer to ask the judgment debtor in addition to those in Form EX140.]

4. [Attached is a list of documents which the judgment creditor wishes the judgment debtor to be ordered to produce in addition to those listed in the note above.]

5. [The judgment creditor requests that the judgment debtor be questioned by the judgment creditor before a judge. The reason for this request is

]

Statement of Truth

*(I believe)(The judgment creditor believes) that the facts stated in this application form are true.
* I am duly authorised by the judgment creditor to sign this statement.

signed __John Smith_____ date __02/06/06_____

*(Judgment creditor)(~~litigation friend~~)(~~judgment creditor's~~)(~~child's~~)(~~parent~~)(Judgment creditor's solicitor)
*delete as appropriate

Full name _____

Name of judgment creditor's solicitor's firm _____

position or office held _____
(if signing on behalf of firm or company)

Judgment creditor's or judgment creditor's solicitor's address to which documents should be sent.	JOHN SMITH 1 THE HIGH STREET LONDON Postcode W1		if applicable
		Ref. no.	
		fax no.	
		DX no.	
	Tel. no. 020 7123 4567	e-mail	

Completed example of Application for Third Party Debt Order Form N349

Application for third party debt order

In the CENTRAL LONDON COUNTY COURT

Claim No. CL4 12345

Appn. No.

JOHN SMITH — Claimant

JAMES SHERBERT — Defendant

ABC BANK LIMITED — Third Party

The [claimant] [defendant] ('the judgment creditor') applies for an order that the third party pay to the judgment creditor the debt which the third party owes to the [defendant] [claimant] ('the judgment debtor') (or so much of it as is necessary to discharge the amount owing under the judgment or order given on 1 JUNE 20 06 [by the CENTRAL LONDON COUNTY COURT in claim no. CL4 12345] and the costs of this application).

1. **Judgment debtor**
   The judgment debtor is JAMES SHERBERT
   whose address is 14 SKINNER HOUSE, WALTHAM ROAD, LONDON

   Postcode SE2 7BX

2. **Judgment debt**
   The judgment or order required the judgment debtor to pay £ 50.00 (including any costs and interest). The amount now due is £ 648.33 [which includes further interest].

   ☐ £ of the instalments due under the judgment or order has fallen due and remains unpaid.

   ☑ The judgment or order did not provide for payment by instalments.

3. **Third party**
   The third party is within England and Wales and owes money to (or holds money to the credit of) the judgment debtor.

   The third party is a bank or building society.
   Its name is ABC BANK LIMITED
   Its head office address in England and Wales is:
   1 LOMBARD ROW, LONDON, EC1

   The branch at which the account is held is
   ☐ not known

   ☑ the ABC BANK LIMITED
   whose address is 22 HIGH STREET, WALTHAM, LONDON SE2

   The account number is
   ☐ not known
   ☑ 012345678

   The sort code is
   ☐ not known
   ☑ 01-00-52

N349 Application for third party debt order (03.02)

(Continued on next page)

Completed example of Application for Third Party Debt Order Form N349
(continued)

[The third party is not a bank or building society.

☐ the third party is

whose address in England and Wales is

4. **Other persons' interests**
   The persons (in addition to the judgment debtor) who have a claim to the money owed by the third party are
   ☑ None

   ☐ The following: *(names and address(es))*

   Information known about each person's claim:

5. **Sources and grounds of information**
   The judgment creditor knowns or believes that the information in section 3 and 4 is correct because:
   THE DEFENDANT'S REPLIES AT ORAL EXAMINATION

6. **Other applications**
   In respect of the judgment debt,
   ☑ the judgment creditor has made no other applications for third party debt orders.
   ☐ the judgment creditor has already made the following application(s) for third party debt order:
   Details of application(s)

   Third party's name
   Address

   Postcode

Statement of Truth
*I believe (the judgment creditor believes) that the facts stated in this application form are true.
*I am duly authorised by the judgment creditor to sign this statement

signed *John Smith* date 30/06/06
*(Judgment creditor)(Litigation friend *where judgment creditor is a child or a patient*)(Judgment creditor's solicitor)
*delete as appropriate
Full name JOHN SMITH
Name of judgment creditor's solicitor's firm _____
position or office held _____ *(if signing on behalf of a firm or company)*

Judgment creditor's or judgment creditor's solicitor's address to which documents should be sent.

JOHN SMITH
1 THE HIGH STREET
LONDON

Postcode   W1

if applicable

Ref. no.	
fax no.	
DX no.	
e-mail	
Tel. no.	020 7123 4567

© 2006 Lawpack Publishing Limited
76-89 Alscot Road, London SE1 3AW
www.lawpack.co.uk

0906428

The DIY Legal Publisher

2006

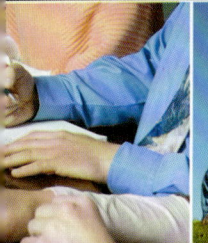

More than two-thirds of people in Britain have not made a Will

Make your Will today with Lawpack's Last Will & Testament Kit
see page 4

Contents

Self-Help Kits	4
Property Books	10
Pocket Guides	16
Made Easy Books	18
Legal and Tax Books	21
When you need it in writing...	26
Form Packs	27
Authors	29
Index	31

Have you made your Will?

If you die without making a Will, your property will be distributed according to law and not necessarily as you would have wished.

By making a Will, you can decide for yourself who is to inherit your estate. This Lawpack Last Will & Testament Kit is valid in England and Wales, Northern Ireland and Scotland. It shows you how to prepare your own Will, easily and legally, without the expense of going to a solicitor.

Guidance manual covers:

- The importance of making a Will and what happens if you die without one
- Occasions and life events after which you should revise your Will
- Choosing and appointing executors to carry out your wishes
- How to give specific gifts and sums of money to beneficiaries
- Appointing guardians and leaving gifts for children
- The residue of your estate and deciding who is to inherit it
- Choosing and completing the Will forms suitable for your circumstances, with completed examples and worksheets
- The procedure for signing your Will correctly in the presence of witnesses

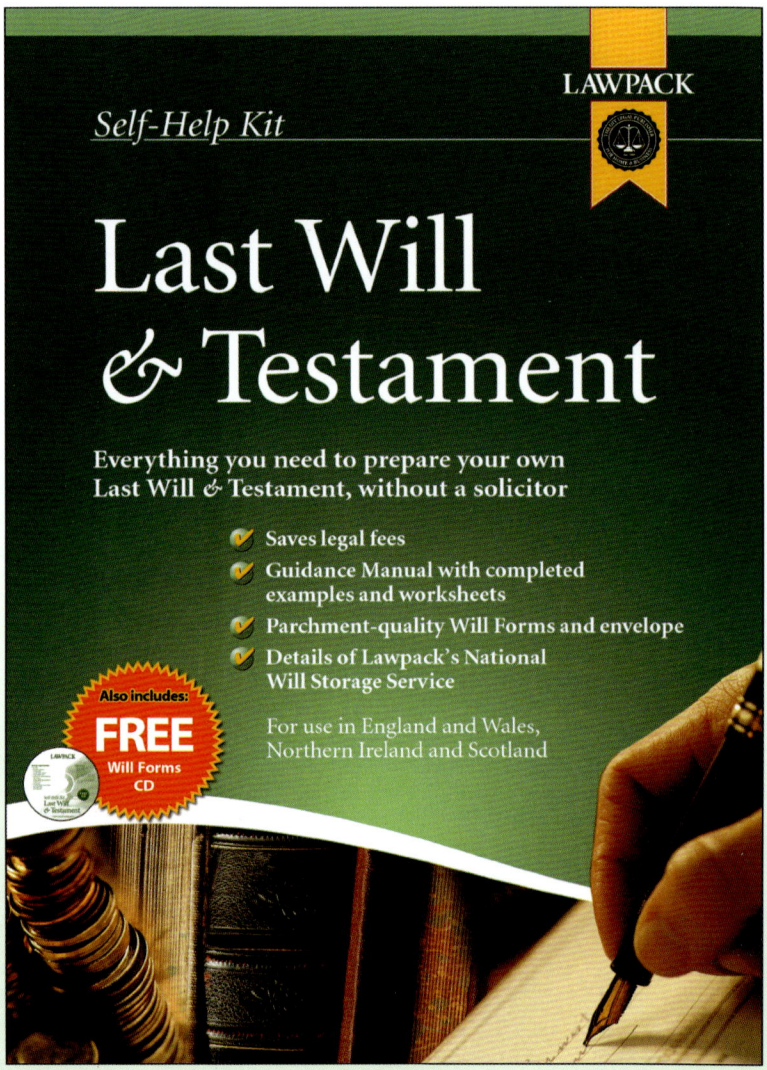

 This Kit is supported online at www.lawpack.co.uk

Approved by Leolin Price QC and Richard Dew, barristers, under English law, by Neill Clerk & Murray solicitors under Scottish law and by John Thompson QC, under the law of Northern Ireland.

CODE	P120	
ISBN	1 904053 53 X	10 DIGIT
ISBN	978 1 904053 53 8	13 DIGIT
SIZE	305 x 220mm Sealed Wallet	
PRICE	£14.99 (zero VAT)	
EDITION	Fourth	
EXTRAS	Includes Free CD	

Self-Help Kits | 5

Helping you prepare for the big day

Are you dreaming of a wonderful wedding day, to herald the beginning of a new and exciting chapter in your life?

This involves very careful planning and you may not feel completely confident about the many choices and decisions you will have to make. If this is so, you will welcome this invaluable Kit to guide you through every organisational detail. Written in a logical, easy-to-use style, this Kit concentrates on the practical aspects of the preparations.

This Kit covers:

- Countdown calendar of all the vital steps at each stage of the preparations
- Planning civil ceremonies and marrying abroad
- Duties of those involved
- Action plans with step-by step sequences to help you organise the transport, flowers, photography and other essentials.
- Checklist workbook, for making sure everything runs smoothly on the day

This Kit is supported online at
www.lawpack.co.uk

CODE	P219	
ISBN	1 905261 13 6	10 DIGIT
ISBN	978 1 905261 13 0	13 DIGIT
SIZE	305 x 220mm Sealed Wallet	
PRICE	£9.99 (zero VAT)	
EDITION	First	

Self-Help Kits

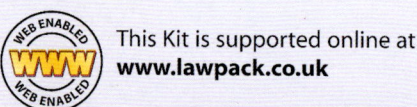

This Kit is supported online at
www.lawpack.co.uk

Approved by Tessa Shepperson, solicitor, under English law and by Neill Clerk & Murray, solicitors, under Scottish law.

Do you want to become a landlord?

Lettings to residential tenants can be a straightforward matter using this Lawpack Residential Letting Kit.

It shows you how to create a legally binding tenancy agreement and includes background information on landlords' and tenants' obligations, rent control, houses in multiple occupation (HMOs), gaining possession of your property, and more. This Kit is for use in situations where the landlord is not resident at the property.

Guidance manual covers:

- Background on Assured Shorthold Tenancies in England & Wales and Short Assured Tenancies in Scotland
- Terms in tenancy agreements
- Houses in multiple occupation (HMOs)
- Inventories and how to avoid disputes over deposits
- Tenants' obligations regarding repairs, outgoings, use of the property, and access for the landlord
- Insurance, safety and structural repair obligations of the landlord
- Rent and how to control it
- Notices to serve before the end of the term or if the tenant falls into rent arrears
- Third party consents, tenants' references and Housing Benefit tenants

CODE	P209	
ISBN	1 904053 96 3	10 DIGIT
ISBN	978 1 904053 96 5	13 DIGIT
SIZE	305 x 220mm Sealed Wallet	
PRICE	£14.99 (zero VAT)	
EDITION	Sixth	
EXTRAS	Includes Free Rent Book	

www.lawpack.co.uk   Self-Help Kits | 7

 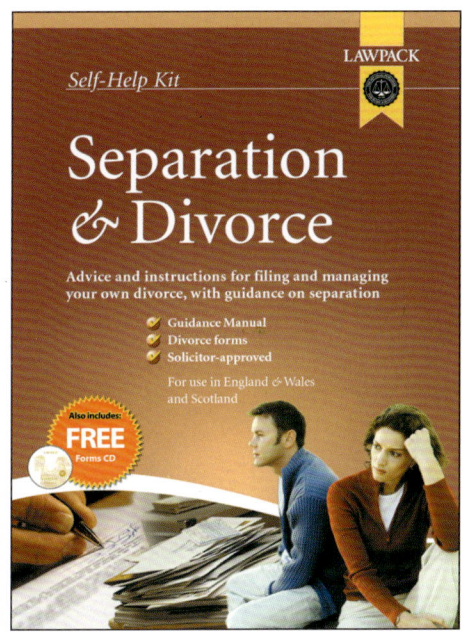 

Power of Attorney Kit   **Separation & Divorce Kit**   **Small Claims Kit**

A power of attorney allows you to authorise someone to act on your behalf with full legal authority. With an increasingly elderly population, the demand for powers of attorney is growing. Creating a power of attorney is straightforward. This Kit includes an Enduring Power of Attorney, a General Power of Attorney (and their Scottish equivalents), and a Guidance Manual with background information and guidance. For use in England & Wales and Scotland.

A divorce does not have to be costly and difficult. This Kit gives you the instructions and information you need to manage your own divorce, without the expense of a solicitor. It explains the legal and financial issues involved and takes you step-by-step from the petition to the final decree. For use in England & Wales and Scotland.

With the help of this Kit you can make a claim using the Small Claims procedure of the County Court, a straightforward and user-friendly way of pursuing a monetary claim of under £5,000. Whether you want to take action to recover a personal debt, resolve a dispute over a business contract or a service provided, or make a claim for damaged property, this Lawpack Kit will show you how. For use in England & Wales.

CODE	P204		CODE	P218		CODE	P208	
ISBN	1 904053 94 7	10 DIGIT	ISBN	1 904053 72 6	10 DIGIT	ISBN	1 904053 95 5	10 DIGIT
ISBN	978 1 904053 94 1	13 DIGIT	ISBN	978 1 904053 72 9	13 DIGIT	ISBN	978 1 904053 95 8	13 DIGIT
SIZE	305 x 220mm Sealed Wallet		SIZE	305 x 220mm Sealed Wallet		SIZE	305 x 220mm Sealed Wallet	
PRICE	£14.99 (zero VAT)		PRICE	£14.99 (zero VAT)		PRICE	£14.99 (zero VAT)	
EDITION	Fourth		EDITION	Second		EDITION	Second	
EXTRAS	Includes Free CD		EXTRAS	Includes Free CD		EXTRAS	Includes Free CD	

Self-Help Kits

Trace your Family Tree Kit

Probate Kit

Sell your own Home Kit

Discovering your family's past can be revealing and absorbing. Genealogy is an increasingly popular pastime and this Kit can help you get started. It contains a Guidance Manual written by experts at the Society of Genealogists that's packed with tips and advice on how and where to begin your researches; it includes all-important sources of further information and details of further reading, template ancestry chart and family group sheets.

CODE	P221	
ISBN	1 905261 30 6	10 DIGIT
ISBN	978 1 905261 30 7	13 DIGIT
SIZE	305 x 220mm Sealed Wallet	
PRICE	£14.99 (zero VAT)	
EDITION	Second	
EXTRAS	Includes Free CD	

After someone dies, with or without leaving a Will, their money, property and belongings need to be dealt with. A grant of probate (or 'Confirmation' in Scotland) is the means by which executors or administrators gain access to the assets of an estate in order to carry out the wishes of the deceased. This Lawpack Kit provides guidance on executors' duties and how to apply for a grant of probate or Confirmation. For use in England & Wales and Scotland.

CODE	P214	
ISBN	1 904053 25 4	10 DIGIT
ISBN	978 1 904053 25 5	13 DIGIT
SIZE	305 x 220mm Sealed Wallet	
PRICE	£14.99 (zero VAT)	
EDITION	First	
EXTRAS	Includes Free CD	

This Lawpack Kit shows you how to prepare your house or flat for sale, how to set the price, market it, arrange viewings, negotiate with buyers and how to clinch the deal.

Whether you decide to use an estate agent or go it alone with a private sale, the 'Sell Your Own Home' Kit guides you through every stage.

CODE	P124	
ISBN	1 904053 80 7	10 DIGIT
ISBN	978 1 904053 80 4	13 DIGIT
SIZE	305 x 220mm Sealed Wallet	
PRICE	£14.99 (zero VAT)	
EDITION	First	
EXTRAS	Includes Free CD	

www.lawpack.co.uk   Self-Help Kits | 9

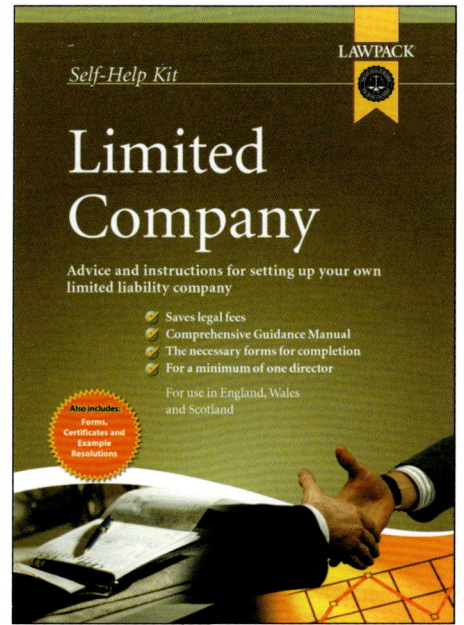

Limited Company Kit   **Employment Contracts Kit**   **Self-Employment Kit**

This Kit explains what a limited company is and provides the documents needed to set one up with a registered office in England, Wales or Scotland. It includes copies of the necessary Companies House forms, Memoranda of Association, Articles of Association, Share Certificates and an instruction manual that guides the reader step-by-step through the process and provides useful background information. For use in England & Wales and Scotland.

This Kit contains what an employer needs in order to prepare contracts for staff and so comply with legal requirements. Full- and part-time, temporary and domestic contracts are included, with a manual that discusses the relevant areas of employment law and the options available to employers and employees. A free CD with contracts and recruitment and management letters is included. For use in England & Wales and Scotland.

Going self-employed is a major decision in life. In effect, you need to meet the demands of running a business yourself. This Kit provides a framework on which to prepare yourself and to develop your own accounting systems. It includes a wealth of practical advice and provides template documents for cashflow, budgets and financial control. For use in England & Wales and Scotland.

CODE	P201		CODE	P210		CODE	P215
ISBN	1 904053 93 9	10 DIGIT	ISBN	1 904053 97 1	10 DIGIT	ISBN	1 904053 99 8	10 DIGIT
ISBN	978 1 904053 93 4	13 DIGIT	ISBN	978 1 904053 97 2	13 DIGIT	ISBN	978 1 904053 99 6	13 DIGIT
SIZE	305 x 220mm Sealed Wallet		SIZE	305 x 220mm Sealed Wallet		SIZE	305 x 220mm Sealed Wallet
PRICE	£14.99 (zero VAT)		PRICE	£14.99 (zero VAT)		PRICE	£14.99 (zero VAT)
EDITION	Sixth		EDITION	Second		EDITION	Second
			EXTRAS	Includes Free CD		EXTRAS	Includes Free CD

Enjoy a place in the sun and make money from your investment

'Jet-to-Let' is the new property phenomenon, as record numbers of people buy property abroad.

In this book, property millionaire Dominic Farrell explains why buying abroad has become such a popular and potentially lucrative investment choice, and why it is forecast to grow year on year. He gives a thorough grounding in the economic indicators that should influence investment decisions. The book features detailed profiles of hotspot countries worldwide, in which the author's financial models are applied and analysed. Dominic is a partner in a large property company. He writes for property investment journals and newspapers and his views are sought by the UK national press and television.

Contents

- Why invest overseas?
- Overseas property investment strategy
- The economics of investing overseas
- The financial issues – what do I need to know?
- Tax and legal considerations
- Risk – how to avoid the pitfalls
- Detailed country-by-country profiles, including Bulgaria, Cyprus, Dubai, Estonia, France, Germany, Hungary, Italy, Morocco, Portugal, Spain, Thailand and the USA (Florida)

CODE	B655	
ISBN	1 905261 11 X	10 DIGIT
ISBN	978 1 905261 11 6	13 DIGIT
SIZE	153 x 234mm PB 560 pages	
PRICE	£14.99	
EDITION	First	
AVAILABLE	June 2006	

Property Books | 11

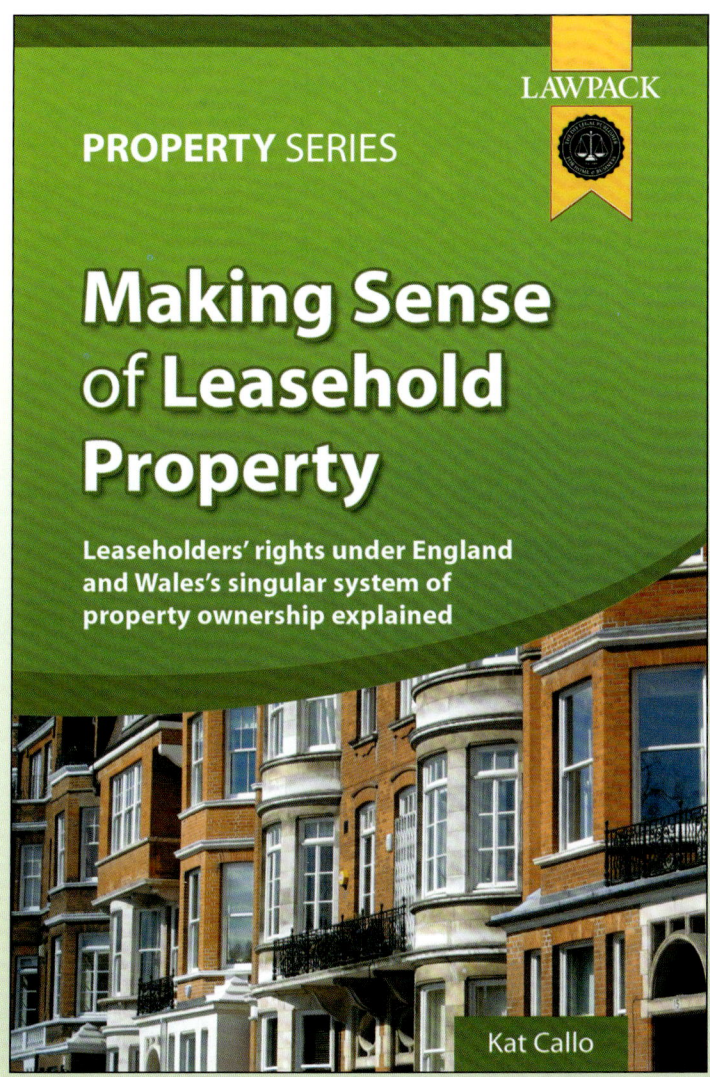

CODE	B438
ISBN	1 904053 12 2 (10 DIGIT)
ISBN	978 1 904053 12 5 (13 DIGIT)
SIZE	153 x 234mm PB 240 pages
PRICE	£11.99
EDITION	First

How can you own your property yet still be a tenant?

A guide to the leasehold and freehold system, providing tips on how to make the best of an imperfect legislative environment that continues to borrow heavily from the feudal age.

The recent boom in residential developments means a growing number of people in England and Wales own leasehold flats. But the laws governing this form of property ownership are complex and antiquated, with some dating back to the feudal age. New legislation now makes it possible for leaseholders to increase the value of their homes by securing greater ownership and control, but options for flat owners can still seem confusing.

Contents

- Disputing your landlord's service charges
- Gaining the right to manage
- Buying the building's freehold through 'collective enfranchisement'
- Negotiated freehold purchases
- Buying a freehold through right of first refusal
- Extending your lease
- Setting up a residents' association
- Case studies and useful contacts
- Template residents' association constitution and enfranchisement notice

'... a unique and valuable guide through the thickets of leasehold law, written in simple and practical terms by a flat owner for flat owners.'

Peter Haler, Chief Executive, Leasehold Advisory Service

Communication skills for landlords

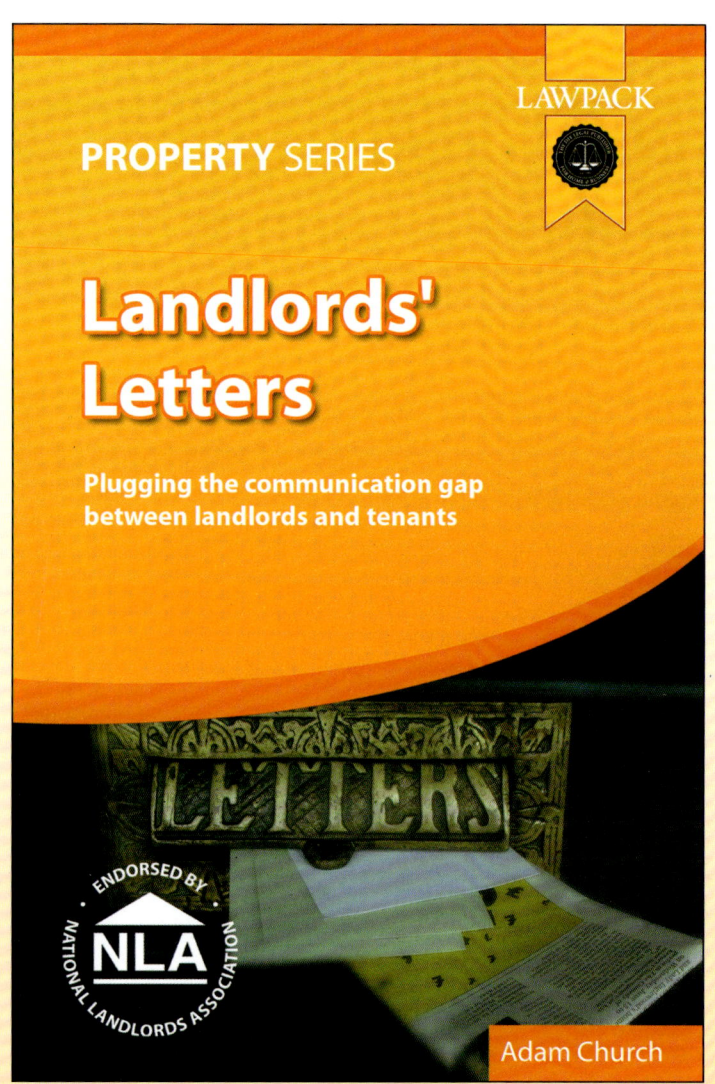

Many of the problems that private landlords encounter are due to poor or ineffective communication with their tenants on the rights and responsibilities of both sides.

Written by property professional Adam Church, this book contains templates for use by landlords of residential property and is accompanied by useful guidance notes on when to send the appropriate letter, or sequential series of letters. It is intended to help landlords in sending clear, accurate information to tenants by mail, so make for successful and trouble-free lettings.

Contents

- Rent arrears
- Gaining access and carrying out repairs
- Complaints to tenants
- Utilities and bills
- Legal notices
- Holiday lets
- Resident landlords
- The deposit

'...an indispensable and easy-to-use reference tool for landlords.'

National Landlords Association

CODE	B652	
ISBN	1 905261 08 X	10 DIGIT
ISBN	978 1 905261 08 6	13 DIGIT
SIZE	153 x 234mm PB 192 pages	
PRICE	£12.99	
EDITION	First	

Buy the freehold and unlock the value of your home

This book answers the questions being asked by growing numbers of flat leaseholders: 'Should we buy our building freehold? If so, how much will it cost, how do we do it and what are the pitfalls to avoid?'

The Commonhold and Leasehold Reform Act made it feasible for long leaseholders to buy their freeholds. But many residents wanting to do so face a David-and-Goliath challenge with landlords who may have deeper pockets, better lawyers, stronger organisational clout and the leisure of time. With clear and simple tools and tips, Lawpack author and leasehold consultant Kat Callo tells you how to go about a successful freehold acquisition without wasting money, time and effort and without souring relationships with your neighbours.

Contents

- Avoiding the stuttering start
- Dealing with documentation
- Demystifying the valuation process
- Preparation, preparation, preparation
- Ready, steady, go!
- Maintaining participant numbers
- Managing opposition
- Negotiate or not?
- Crossing the finishing line
- Beating burn-out
- Appendices

CODE	B654	
ISBN	1 905261 10 1	10 DIGIT
ISBN	978 1 905261 10 9	13 DIGIT
SIZE	153 x 234mm PB 160 pages	
PRICE	£11.99	
EDITION	First	
AVAILABLE	July 2006	

Property Books

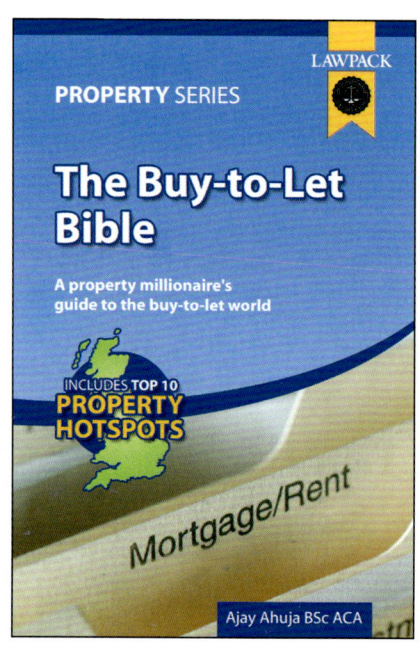  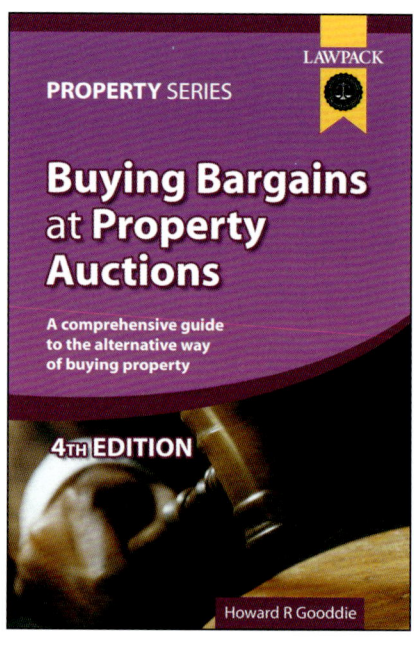

The Buy-to-Let Bible
Ajay Ahuja

Residential Lettings
Tessa Shepperson

Buying Bargains at Property Auctions
Howard Gooddie

Low mortgage rates and continued under-performance by traditional savings and investment products means that property still looks a better way to invest for the future. Author Ajay Ahuja divulges the practical and financial techniques that have made him a millionaire. It covers finding the right property, the right mortgage lender, the right tenant, legal issues and tax. Buy-to-let property 'hotspots' by region across the UK are also listed.

Are you thinking of letting a flat or a house? This guide steers anyone who intends – or already is – letting property through the legal and practical issues involved. It provides all the up-to-date information and tips that a would-be landlord needs. It will also alert existing landlords to the points of good practice that make a letting successful, and the legal obligations that they may not be aware of. For lettings in England & Wales and Scotland.

Every week, hundreds of commercial and residential properties are sold at auction in Britain, often at bargain prices, with owner-occupiers accounting for a growing proportion of buyers. In this bestselling guide, author and property auctioneer Howard Gooddie spells out how straightforward the auction route can be and divulges the tips and practices of this relatively unknown world.

CODE	B637		CODE	B622		CODE	B626	
ISBN	1 904053 91 2	10 DIGIT	ISBN	1 904053 90 4	10 DIGIT	ISBN	1 904053 89 0	10 DIGIT
ISBN	978 1 904053 91 0	13 DIGIT	ISBN	978 1 904053 90 3	13 DIGIT	ISBN	978 1 904053 89 7	13 DIGIT
SIZE	153 x 234mm PB 256 pages		SIZE	153 x 234mm PB 160 pages		SIZE	153 x 234mm PB 304 pages	
PRICE	£11.99		PRICE	£11.99		PRICE	£11.99	
EDITION	Third		EDITION	Fifth		EDITION	Fourth	

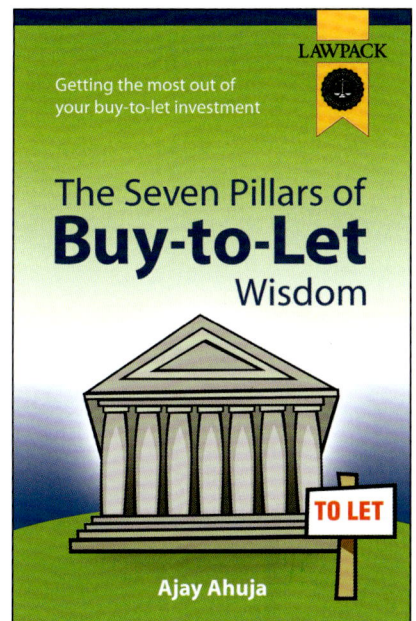 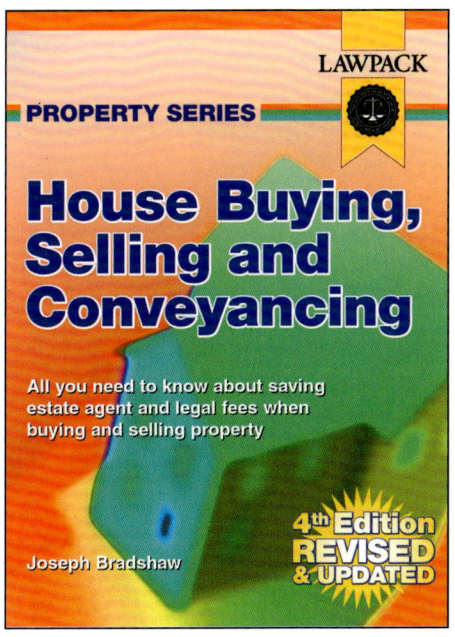 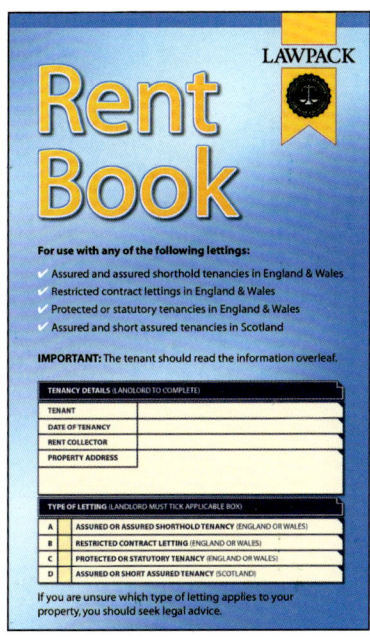

The Seven Pillars of Buy-to-Let Wisdom
Ajay Ahuja

In his first, bestselling buy-to-let book, *The Buy-to-Let Bible* author and buy-to-let millionaire Ajay Ahuja provided the basics of successful buy-to-let. Ajay has now written 'further reading' for the buy-to-let investor, *The Seven Pillars of Buy-to-let Wisdom*, that explains in depth how to get the most from your investment by examining the seven fundamentals of successful buy-to-let property management.

CODE	B447
ISBN	1 904053 42 4 10 DIGIT
ISBN	978 1 904053 42 2 13 DIGIT
SIZE	153 x 234mm PB 144 pages
PRICE	£9.99
EDITION	First

House Buying, Selling and Conveyancing
Joseph Bradshaw

This Lawpack Guide is intended for those who want to cut out the solicitor and estate agent middlemen when buying and selling a house. The author, Joseph Bradshaw, tells you how straightforward it is, in a witty, down-to-earth style. This is the fourth Lawpack edition – revised in line with Land Registration Act changes – of the original Bradshaw guide, which earned the author the description 'the guru of layperson conveyancing' in *The Times*. For use in England & Wales.

CODE	B412
ISBN	1 904053 61 0 10 DIGIT
ISBN	978 1 904053 61 3 13 DIGIT
SIZE	153 x 234mm PB 160 pages
PRICE	£11.99
EDITION	Fourth

Rent Book

The Lawpack 'all-in-one' Rent Book has been specially prepared for use with all the commonly occurring types of letting: assured and assured shorthold tenancies, restricted contract lettings and protected or statutory tenancies in England & Wales, and assured and short assured tenancies in Scotland. It includes the notices and information for tenants for each type of letting. Required by law when rent is paid on a weekly basis.

CODE	RB002
ISBN	1 904053 24 6 10 DIGIT
ISBN	978 1 904053 24 8 13 DIGIT
SIZE	170 x 100mm PB 16 pages
PRICE	£1.99
EDITION	First

How to live and work under the same roof

Can I get a Council Tax reduction if I work from home?

What are my employer's health and safety obligations if I become a homeworker?

What expenses can I claim if I run my business from home?

This pocket book provides quick answers to these and other questions asked by the growing number of people working from home, either self-employed or as homeworkers. Author Hugh Williams provides a useful overview of the legal and tax implications of working from home. He warns of the pitfalls to beware of and encourages you to make the most of all the opportunities that working from home presents.

Contents

- Tax rates and allowances
- Some popular ways of earning money from home
- Rules and regulations
- You and your customers
- The employed at home
- Sample full business plan
- Specimen layout for a set of accounts
- Business partnership agreement between husband and wife
- Health and safety - the elementary steps that should be taken by an employer when an employee works from home
- Valid in England & Wales and Scotland.

CODE	B105	
ISBN	1 904053 79 3	10 DIGIT
ISBN	978 1 904053 79 8	13 DIGIT
SIZE	190 x 105mm PB 96 pages	
PRICE	£3.99	
EDITION	First	

Pocket Guides

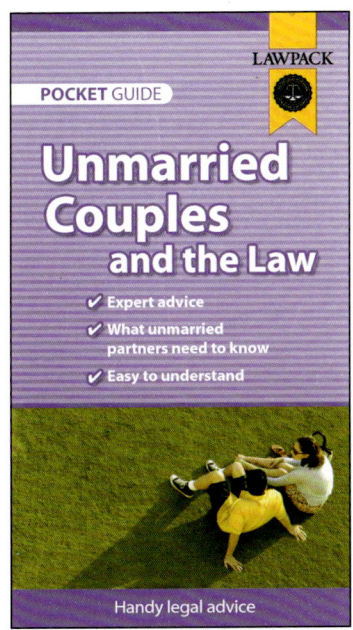

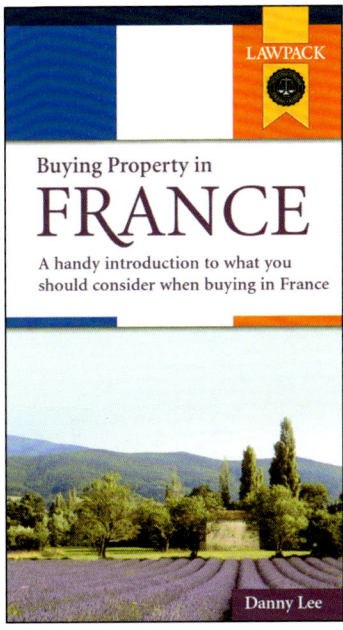

Unmarried Couples and the Law
Phillipa Pearson

What rights do an unmarried couple have over joint finances?

Who is legally responsible for the children?

And what happens to property if a couple split up?

Living together raises a variety of important legal questions that apply to the growing number of couples who choose not to marry. Find out the answers in this book. Valid in England & Wales and Scotland.

CODE	B103	
ISBN	1 904053 82 3	10 DIGIT
ISBN	978 1 904053 82 8	13 DIGIT
SIZE	190 x 105mm PB 112 pages	
PRICE	£3.99	
EDITION	First	

Your Rights at Work
Melanie Slocombe

Does an employer have to give an employee a written contract?

What time off is an employee allowed?

Can an employee be made redundant if she becomes pregnant?

This book provides quick answers to these and many other important employment law questions. Valid in England & Wales and Scotland.

CODE	B104	
ISBN	1 904053 83 1	10 DIGIT
ISBN	978 1 904053 83 5	13 DIGIT
SIZE	190 x 105mm PB 96 pages	
PRICE	£3.99	
EDITION	First	

Buying Property in France
Danny Lee

Many of us dream of owning property in France. This pocket guide provides a quick and convenient overview of the realities and practicalities of buying a property in France, and what you should consider before embarking on your dream.

It highlights the important things that you as a would-be purchaser must consider, whether it's buying a property as a second home or for letting it as a business.

CODE	B449	
ISBN	1 904053 74 2	10 DIGIT
ISBN	978 1 904053 74 3	13 DIGIT
SIZE	190 x 105mm PB 112 pages	
PRICE	£4.99	
EDITION	First	

Business entry and exit, from the corner shop to the Square Mile

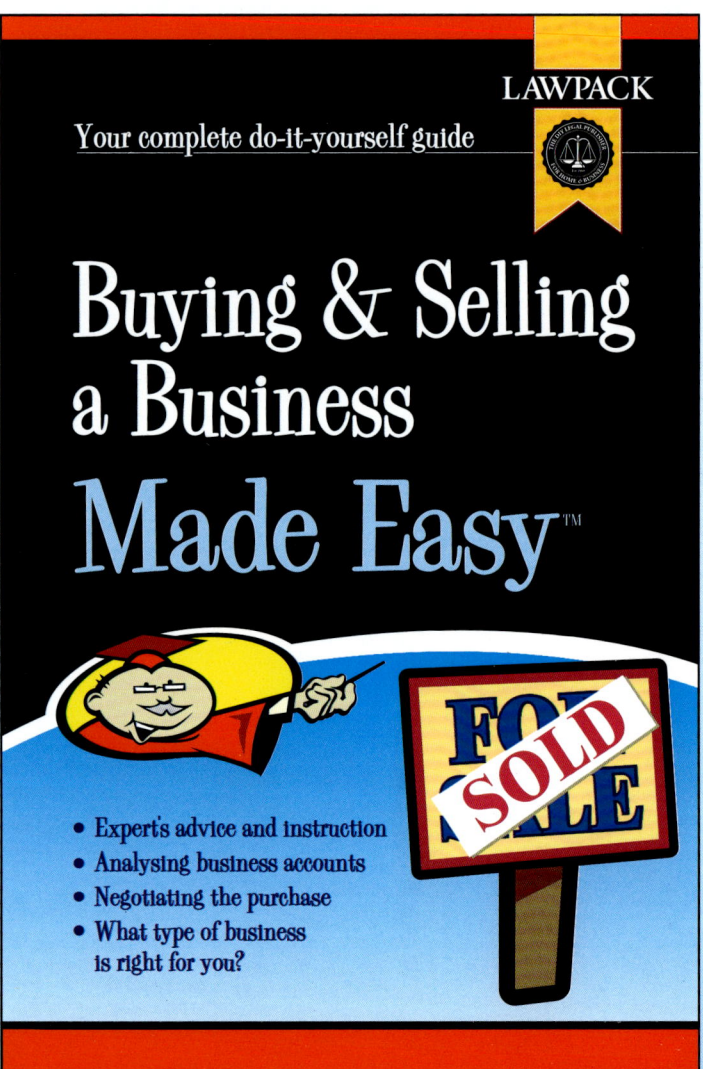

A guide for owners or managers of private companies who want a readable overview of the principles and mechanics of buying and selling small- and medium-sized businesses (SMEs).

You don't need an MBA to understand the fundamentals of buying and selling a business, just a sound working knowledge of business principles. Author Hugh Williams takes a detailed look at both the buy and sell side and guides the reader through the different stages of the processes involved and the vital financial considerations and other judgements to be made.

Contents

- What type of business is right for you?
- Comparing the range of business sectors
- Appraising the business of your choice
- How much should you pay?
- Negotiating the purchase of your chosen business
- Finding the funds to complete the purchase
- Selling a business
- Case studies and template documents

CODE	B721	
ISBN	1 905261 22 5	10 DIGIT
ISBN	978 1 905261 22 2	13 DIGIT
SIZE	153 x 234mm PB 240 pages	
PRICE	£10.99	
EDITION	First	
AVAILABLE	October 2006	

www.lawpack.co.uk Made Easy Books | 19

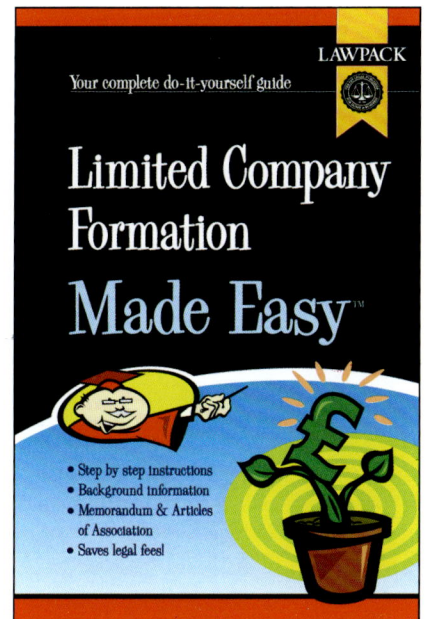

Limited Company Formation Made Easy

Incorporation as a limited liability company is the preferred structure for thousands of successful businesses. This guide explains why, and shows you how to set up your own limited liability company easily and inexpensively. It provides detailed but easy to follow instructions, background information, completed examples of Companies House forms and drafts of other necessary documents.

CODE	B703	
ISBN	1 904053 98 X	10 DIGIT
ISBN	978 1 904053 98 9	13 DIGIT
SIZE	153 x 234mm PB 128 pages	
PRICE	£11.99	
EDITION	Second	

Employment Law Made Easy
Melanie Slocombe

Written by an employment law solicitor, *Employment Law Made Easy* is a comprehensive, reader-friendly source of information that will provide answers to practically all your employment law questions. Essential knowledge for employers and employees. Valid for use throughout the UK.

CODE	B702	
ISBN	1 904053 88 2	10 DIGIT
ISBN	978 1 904053 88 0	13 DIGIT
SIZE	153 x 234mm PB 224 pages	
PRICE	£11.99	
EDITION	Sixth	

Business Agreements Made Easy
Yvette Hoskings-James

This book provides the basics on business-to-business contracts for the supply of services and/or goods, and provides suggested actions and steps to guide anyone who has to review or draft contracts and terms of trade for their business.

It explains the key commercial and legal issues which occur throughout a 'contract lifecycle', from pre-contract stage to negotiation and through to the end of a contract.

CODE	B519	
ISBN	1 904053 84 X	10 DIGIT
ISBN	978 1 904053 84 2	13 DIGIT
SIZE	153 x 234mm PB 144 pages	
PRICE	£11.99	
EDITION	First	

Made Easy Books

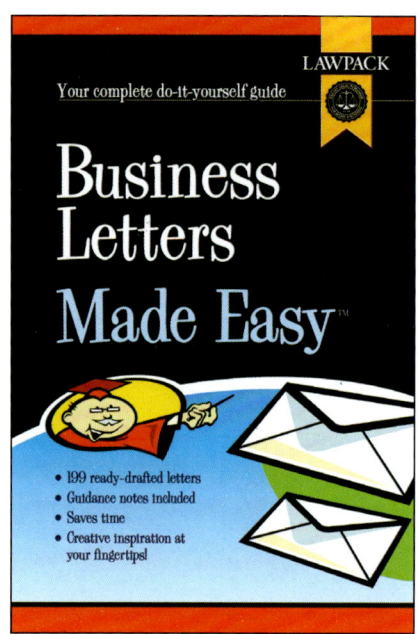

Business Letters Made Easy

When a typical letter can cost a business approximately £15 to send out, mostly in the time of the manager composing it, anything that can bring the cost down will make a big difference. This Made Easy Guide is an asset to saving time and money. All the letters in this book may be copied straight from the page, and some will require only a slight amendment.

CODE	B520	
ISBN	1 904053 87 4	10 DIGIT
ISBN	978 1 904053 87 3	13 DIGIT
SIZE	153 x 234mm PB 288 pages	
PRICE	£12.99	
EDITION	First	

Book-Keeping Made Easy
Roy Hedges

Many businesses fail in their first year or two because of insufficient financial control. This guide provides the new business owner with an understanding of the fundamental principles of book-keeping, showing how to set up accounts and how to benefit from the information they contain. Includes procedures for the sole proprietor and small business, accounting for growing businesses, double-entry book-keeping, ledgers, payroll and final accounts.

CODE	B716	
ISBN	1 904053 85 8	10 DIGIT
ISBN	978 1 904053 85 9	13 DIGIT
SIZE	153 x 234mm PB 104 pages	
PRICE	£10.99	
EDITION	Second	

Running your own Business Made Easy
Roy Hedges

You have a business idea that you want to put into action, but you also want advice on the realities of setting up and running a business: this Made Easy guide is for you. It takes you through the business-creation process, from assessing your aptitude and ideas, to funding and business plans.

CODE	B711	
ISBN	1 905261 05 5	10 DIGIT
ISBN	978 1 905261 05 5	13 DIGIT
SIZE	153 x 234mm PB 192 pages	
PRICE	£10.99	
EDITION	Third	

Plan ahead and save your family from the 'voluntary tax'

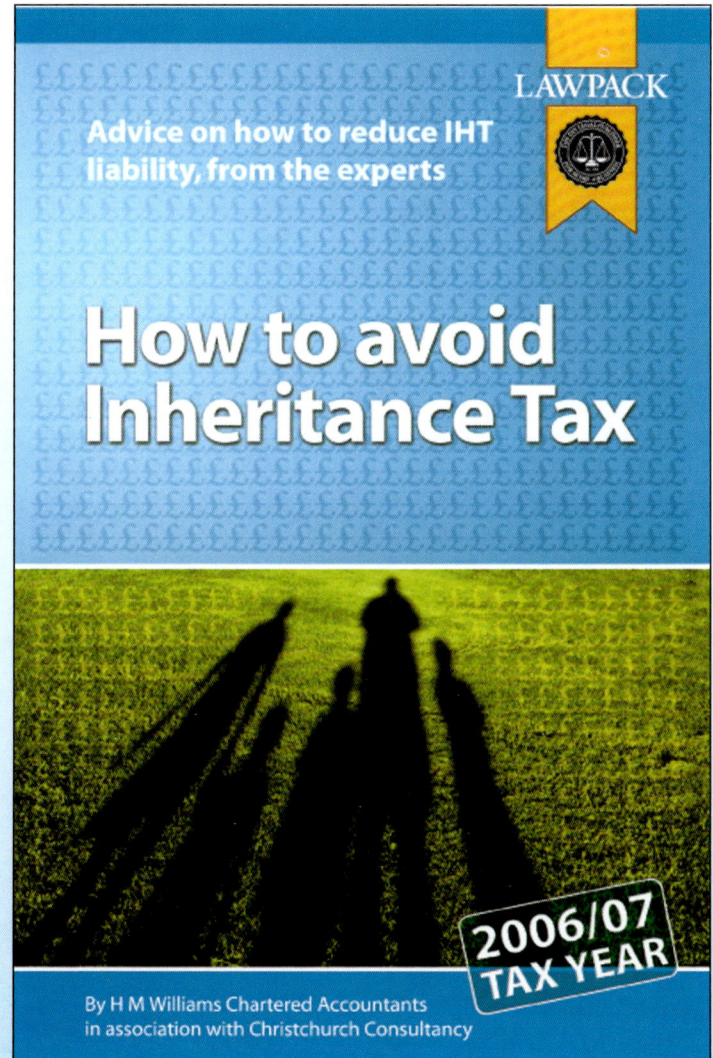

CODE	B653
ISBN	1 905261 09 8 — 10 DIGIT
ISBN	978 1 905261 09 3 — 13 DIGIT
SIZE	153 x 234mm PB
PRICE	£9.99
EDITION	First
AVAILABLE	September 2006

As property prices have risen, so has the likelihood that the value of your estate will exceed the Inheritance Tax (IHT) threshold.

IHT is in effect a voluntary tax, in that you can take measures to reduce your liability, in some cases to nil, and so pass on your money and property to your family or friends after your death, rather than letting it go to HM Treasury.

This book has been written by Hugh Williams award-winning Chartered Accountant and bestselling author of Lawpack's *Tax Answers at Glance* in association with IHT specialists Christchurch Consultancy. It explains what steps and measures you can take to reduce your IHT liability.

Contents

- An outline of IHT
- Working out the value of your estate
- Planning your Will
- Calculating the size of your IHT bill
- Assets that attract relief
- Ways to reduce your IHT bill
- Trusts and their uses
- Traps to be aware of
- What to do with certain types of asset
- Putting an IHT mitigation exercise into effect
- How life assurance can help reduce the impact of IHT

Legal and Tax Books

www.lawpack.co.uk

101 Ways to Pay Less Tax
HM Williams

Tax Answers at a Glance
HM Williams

Trip and Slip
Felicity Mileham
ed. Henmans Solicitors

This book provides a wealth of tax saving tips from H M Williams Chartered Accountants, a national award winning firm of chartered accountants.

The tips included in this book are all legitimate ways to help reduce your tax bill - tax avoidance rather than tax evasion. It provides advice for low and high earners, pensioners, employees and employers and more.

Lower your tax bill with this book of easy-to-follow hints from a team of highly regarded chartered accountants.

This book provides a wealth of tax saving tips from H M Williams Chartered Accountants, a national award winning firm of chartered accountants.

The tips included in this book are all legitimate ways to help reduce your tax bill - tax avoidance rather than tax evasion.

Many people are not aware of the compensation that may be available to them as a result of injury at work, play, on the road, from a defective product, or through medical negligence. This guide sets out what losses you may claim for, how to collect evidence, how the court procedure works and what sums of money the courts award. It also provides guidance on what defences are available, should someone be making a claim against you. For use in England & Wales.

CODE	B648	
ISBN	1 905261 21 7	10 DIGIT
ISBN	978 1 905261 21 5	13 DIGIT
SIZE	153 x 234mm PB 160 pages	
PRICE	£9.99	
EDITION	Second	
AVAILABLE	April 2006	

CODE	B625	
ISBN	1 905261 20 9	10 DIGIT
ISBN	978 1 905261 20 8	13 DIGIT
SIZE	153 x 234mm PB 240 pages	
PRICE	£9.99	
EDITION	Sixth	
AVAILABLE	April 2006	

CODE	B424	
ISBN	1 904053 68 8	10 DIGIT
ISBN	978 1 904053 68 2	13 DIGIT
SIZE	153 x 234mm PB 240 pages	
PRICE	£11.99	
EDITION	Second	

www.lawpack.co.uk

Legal and Tax Books | 23

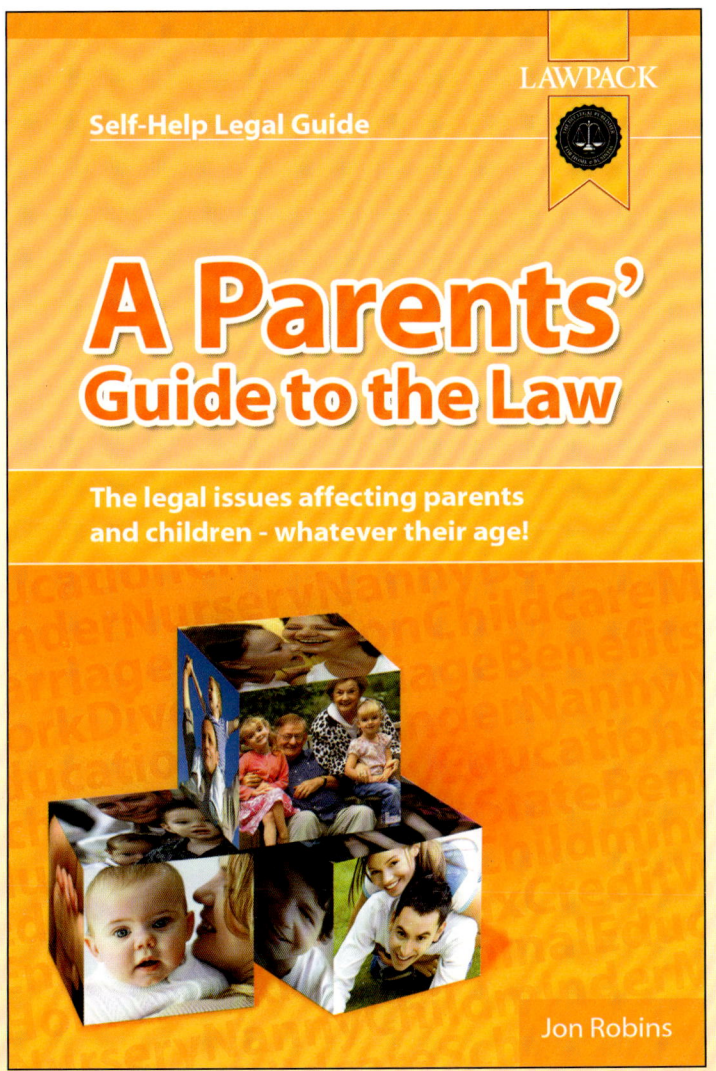

Legal schooling for parents

What are your rights as a parent?

And what are those of your children?

What standards can you expect from schools, hospitals and other services that provide for you and your family?

This book by award-winning legal journalist Jon Robins will draw parents' attention to the many ways the law affects family life. From birth and parental responsibility through to grandparenting, it will help parents know where they stand by highlighting key issues.

Contents

- Parental responsibility: what it means to be a parent
- Becoming a parent
- Childcare: pre-school
- Education: choosing the right school
- Education: school-life
- Money and work
- Separation and divorce
- Grandparents

CODE	B656	
ISBN	1 905261 19 5	10 DIGIT
ISBN	978 1 905261 19 2	13 DIGIT
SIZE	153 x 234mm PB 240 pages	
PRICE	£10.99	
EDITION	First	
AVAILABLE	February 2007	

Legal and Tax Books

www.lawpack.co.uk

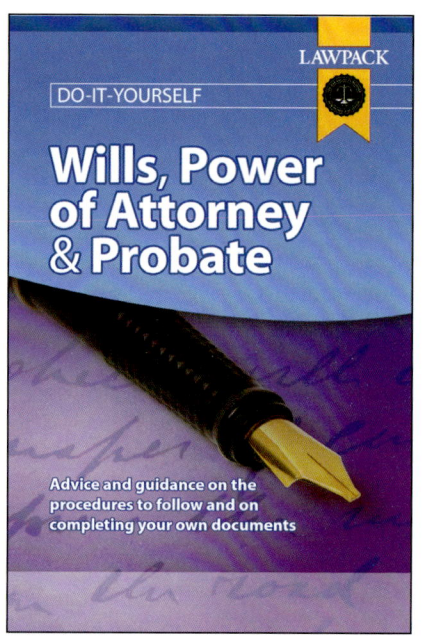

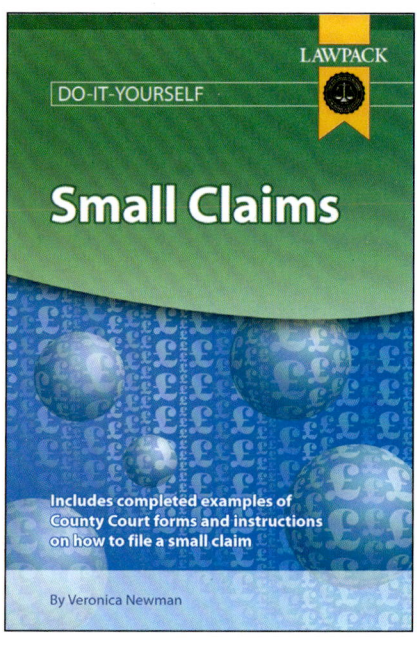

Employment Law
Melanie Slocombe

Wills, Power of Attorney & Probate
ed. Richard Dew

Small Claims
Veronica Newman

Whether you are an employer or an employee, you have ever-increasing rights and duties in the workplace. This bestselling guide is a comprehensive source of up-to-date knowledge on hiring, wages, employment contracts, family-friendly rights, discrimination, termination and other important issues. It puts at your fingertips the important legal points that all employers and employees should know about. For use throughout the UK.

This guide combines three closely related areas of law; in a Will, you set out whom is to inherit your 'estate'; a power of attorney authorises another to act on your behalf with full legal authority; and via probate (or 'Confirmation' in Scotland), executors gain authority to administer your Will. This guide provides comprehensive background information and step-by-step instructions. For use in England & Wales and Scotland.

If you want to take action to recover a debt, resolve a contract dispute or make a personal injury claim, you can file your own small claim without a solicitor. This guide includes clear instructions and advice on how to handle your own case and enforce judgment. For use in England & Wales.

CODE	B608	CODE	B607	CODE	B606
ISBN	1 904053 92 0 10 DIGIT	ISBN	1 905261 07 1 10 DIGIT	ISBN	1 904053 75 0 10 DIGIT
ISBN	978 1 904053 92 7 13 DIGIT	ISBN	978 1 905261 07 9 13 DIGIT	ISBN	978 1 904053 75 0 13 DIGIT
SIZE	153 x 234mm PB 224 pages	SIZE	153 x 234mm PB 256 pages	SIZE	153 x 234mm PB 180 pages
PRICE	£11.99	PRICE	£11.99	PRICE	£11.99
EDITION	Eighth	EDITION	Second	EDITION	Third
		AVAILABLE	July 2006	AVAILABLE	September 2006

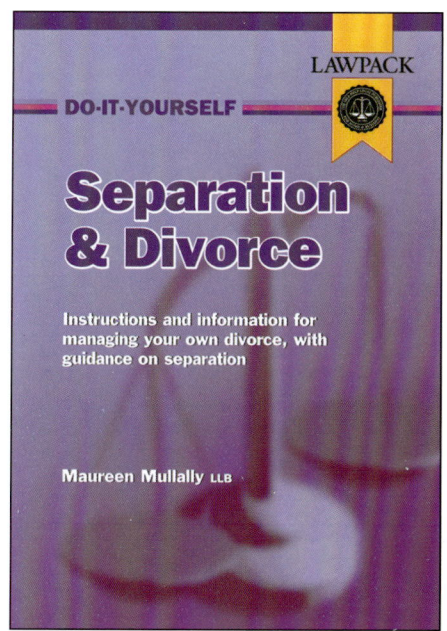

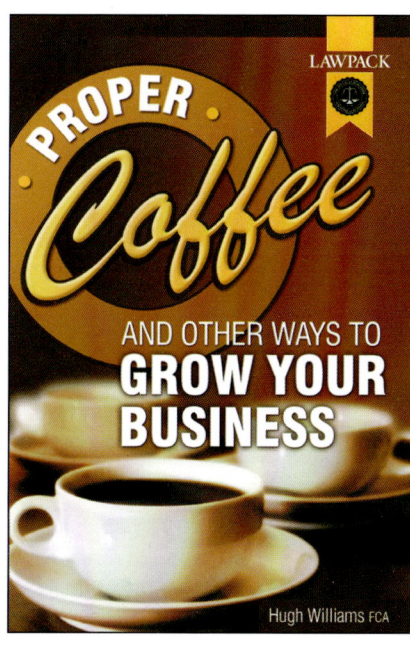

Separation & Divorce
Maureen Mullally

Health and Safety at Work Essentials
Henmans Solicitors

Proper Coffee and Other Ways to Grow your Business
Hugh Williams

Splitting up does not have to be costly and difficult. This guide discusses the practicalities of separation and gives advice on managing your own divorce. The legal and financial issues are explained, and advice given on how to care for and maintain contact with children after divorce and on crisis situations, such as domestic violence and child abduction.

Every workplace has to comply with an extensive range of health and safety rules and regulations. With more legal claims being made daily, the price for failing to comply, whether through fines or claims by employees, can be high. This is a handy, 'one-stop' handbook for anyone responsible for health and safety issues in the workplace. It sets out the background legal basics and provides succinct, practical advice on what measures to take.

Why proper coffee? Because often it's the small things, such as offering proper coffee to customers and clients, that get a business noticed, and create a lasting impression and worthy reputation. Turgid business tomes abound. As an alternative, Hugh Williams, award-winning chartered accountant and business adviser, offers a personal approach to the simple ways in which a small business can win over customers and grow, without working that much harder.

CODE	B445	
ISBN	1 904053 32 7	10 DIGIT
ISBN	978 1 904053 32 3	13 DIGIT
SIZE	153 x 234mm PB 224 pages	
PRICE	£11.99	
EDITION	First	

CODE	B635	
ISBN	1 905261 24 1	10 DIGIT
ISBN	978 1 905261 24 6	13 DIGIT
SIZE	153 x 234mm PB 184 pages	
PRICE	£9.99	
EDITION	Fifth	

CODE	B451	
ISBN	1 904053 86 6	10 DIGIT
ISBN	978 1 904053 86 6	13 DIGIT
SIZE	153 x 234mm PB 128 pages	
PRICE	£9.99	
EDITION	First	

When you need it in writing...

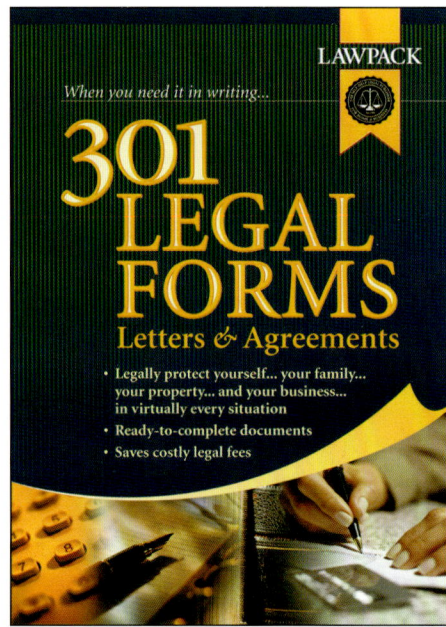
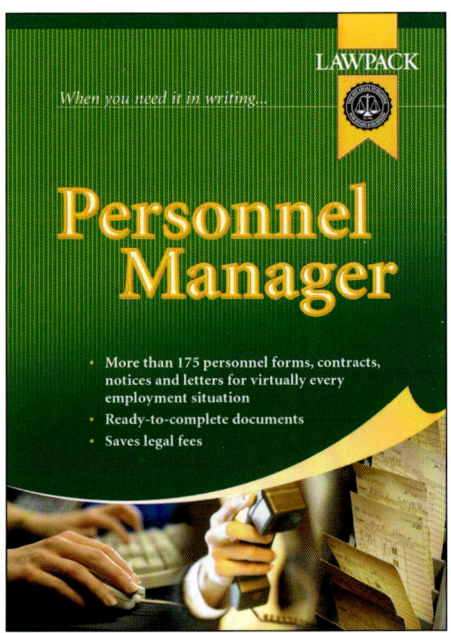

Ready-Made Company Minutes & Resolutions

This book is what every time-pressed company secretary or record-keeper needs. Maintaining good, up-to-date records of company meetings and resolutions is not only good practice but also a legal requirement, whatever size your company is. This book of forms makes compiling minutes of board and shareholder meetings straightforward. It includes more than 125 commonly-required resolutions and minutes to save you time and effort.

CODE	B616	
ISBN	1 904053 73 4	10 DIGIT
ISBN	978 1 904053 73 6	13 DIGIT
SIZE	210 x 297mm PB 184 pages	
PRICE	£14.99	
EDITION	Third	

301 Legal Forms, Letters & Agreements

Our best-selling form book is now in its eighth edition. It is packed with forms, letters and agreements for legal protection in many situations. It provides a complete do-it-yourself library of 301 ready-to-use legal documents, for business or personal use. Areas covered include loans and borrowing, buying and selling, employment, transfers and assignments and residential tenancy.

CODE	B402	
ISBN	1 904053 66 1	10 DIGIT
ISBN	978 1 904053 66 8	13 DIGIT
SIZE	210 x 297mm PB 384 pages	
PRICE	£19.99	
EDITION	Eighth	

Personnel Manager

As employment law and codes of practice increasingly affect the workplace, good, efficient, record-keeping is essential for any employer, large or small.

Personnel Manager is a book of template letters and documents that can help you legally document your important personnel agreements and comply with legal obligations

CODE	B417	
ISBN	1 905261 04 7	10 DIGIT
ISBN	978 1 905261 04 8	13 DIGIT
SIZE	210 x 297mm PB 256 pages	
PRICE	£14.99	
EDITION	Fourth	

Form Packs

Prepare your own everyday legal forms quickly and inexpensively and save legal fees.

Two forms for England & Wales and two for Scotland, plus completed examples and basic instructions, are included. Solicitor-approved.

England & Wales and Scotland

Furnished House/Flat Rental Agreement
A tenancy agreement for letting furnished property on an Assured Shorthold Tenancy for England & Wales or a Short Assured Tenancy for Scotland.

CODE	F301	
ISBN	1 905261 00 4	10 DIGIT
ISBN	978 1 905261 00 0	13 DIGIT
PRICE	£4.49	

House/Flat Share Agreement (Non-Resident Owner)
An agreement for letting a room on an Assured Shorthold Tenancy for England & Wales or a Short Assured Tenancy for Scotland with a non-resident owner.

CODE	F304	
ISBN	1 905261 06 3	10 DIGIT
ISBN	978 1 902646 06 2	13 DIGIT
PRICE	£4.49	

Lodger Agreement
A standard agreement for letting a room in a furnished house or flat with a resident owner, in which common parts of the property (e.g. bathroom, lavatory, kitchen and sitting room) are shared.

CODE	F303	
ISBN	1 905261 02 0	10 DIGIT
ISBN	978 1 905261 02 4	13 DIGIT
PRICE	£4.49	

Household Inventory
Keep a record of the contents of a property and enclose it with the rental agreement.

CODE	F308	
ISBN	1 898217 32 7	10 DIGIT
ISBN	978 1 898217 32 9	13 DIGIT
PRICE	£4.49	

Notice to Terminate
A statutory notice that can be used by a landlord wanting to gain possession of a property at the end of an Assured Shorthold Tenancy (in England & Wales) or a Short Assured Tenancy (in Scotland).

ODE	F306	
ISBN	1 905261 03 9	10 DIGIT
ISBN	978 1 905261 03 1	13 DIGIT
PRICE	£4.49	

Unfurnished House/Flat Rental Agreement
A standard agreement for letting unfurnished property on an Assured Shorthold Tenancy for England & Wales or a Short Assured Tenancy for Scotland.

CODE	F302	
ISBN	1 905261 01 2	10 DIGIT
ISBN	978 1 905261 01 7	13 DIGIT
PRICE	£4.49	

England & Wales

Anti-Gazumping Agreement
A contract between a buyer and seller of a property, which prevents the seller from dealing with other prospective buyers.

CODE	F214	
ISBN	1 898217 58 0	10 DIGIT
ISBN	978 1 898217 58 9	13 DIGIT
PRICE	£4.49	

Builder/Decorator Contract
An agreement suitable for a domestic appointment of a builder or decorator.

CODE	F210	
ISBN	1 898217 42 4	10 DIGIT
ISBN	978 1 898217 42 8	13 DIGIT
PRICE	£4.49	

Business Partnership Agreement
An agreement to govern the creation and management of a business partnership.

CODE	F211	
ISBN	1 902646 15 0	10 DIGIT
ISBN	978 1 902646 15 2	13 DIGIT
PRICE	£4.49	

Cohabitation Agreement
An agreement between partners covering the possessions and the responsibilities within their relationship.

CODE	F217	
ISBN	1 898217 73 4	10 DIGIT
ISBN	978 1 898217 73 2	13 DIGIT
PRICE	£4.49	

Form Packs

Employment Contract
Create a contract between two parties to govern the terms of employment.

CODE	F209	
ISBN	1 902646 11 8	10 DIGIT
ISBN	978 1 902646 11 4	13 DIGIT
PRICE	£4.49	

General Power of Attorney
Authorise somebody to act on your behalf in important legal matters.

CODE	F220	
ISBN	1 902646 16 9	10 DIGIT
ISBN	978 1 902646 16 9	13 DIGIT
PRICE	£4.49	

Holiday Letting Agreement
Agreements for letting out a furnished property for a holiday.

CODE	F213	
ISBN	1 898217 53 X	10 DIGIT
ISBN	978 1 898217 53 4	13 DIGIT
PRICE	£4.49	

Living Will
An advance declaration of your wishes about medical treatments which you could be given for any future illness, which you may not be able to communicate yourself at the relevant time because of physical or mental incapacity.

CODE	F212	
ISBN	1 898217 52 1	10 DIGIT
ISBN	978 1 898217 52 7	13 DIGIT
PRICE	£4.49	

Pools Syndicate Agreement
Bring certainty to your pools syndicate arrangements.

CODE	F219	
ISBN	1 898217 83 1	10 DIGIT
ISBN	978 1 898217 83 1	13 DIGIT
PRICE	£4.49	

Sales Representative Agreement
An agreement governing the relationship between a sales representative and employer.

CODE	F218	
ISBN	1 898217 78 5	10 DIGIT
ISBN	978 1 898217 78 7	13 DIGIT
PRICE	£4.49	

Share Certificate
A share certificate that can be used by a company limited by shares, a company limited by guarantee with a share capital, or an unlimited company with a share capital.

CODE	F222	
ISBN	1 904053 02 5	10 DIGIT
ISBN	978 1 904053 02 6	13 DIGIT
PRICE	£4.49	

Stock Transfer
A form for transferring the legal ownership of shares in a company.

CODE	F223	
ISBN	1 902646 99 1	10 DIGIT
ISBN	978 1 902646 99 2	13 DIGIT
PRICE	£4.49	

Vehicle Purchase Agreement
Create a contract for the private sale of a vehicle.

CODE	F221	
ISBN	1 902646 31 2	10 DIGIT
ISBN	978 1 902646 31 2	13 DIGIT
PRICE	£4.49	

Scotland

Business Partnership Agreement
A contract between individuals starting a business partnership in Scotland.

CODE	SF211	
ISBN	1 898217 64 5	10 DIGIT
ISBN	978 1 898217 64 0	13 DIGIT
PRICE	£4.49	

Employment Contract
An agreement covering an employment relationship in Scotland.

CODE	SF209	
ISBN	1 898217 59 9	10 DIGIT
ISBN	978 1 898217 59 6	13 DIGIT
PRICE	£4.49	

General Power of Attorney
A statutory form enabling an individual to authorise someone else to act on the his or her behalf and in his or her name in Scotland.

CODE	SF220	
ISBN	1 898217 69 6	10 DIGIT
ISBN	978 1 898217 69 5	13 DIGIT
PRICE	£4.49	

Holiday Letting Agreement
Agreements for letting out a furnished property for a holiday for Scotland.

CODE	SF213	
ISBN	1 898217 44 0	10 DIGIT
ISBN	978 1 898217 44 2	13 DIGIT
PRICE	£4.49	

Notice of a Short Assured Tenancy
A statutory notice providing background information for both landlord and tenant, which must be used with a Scottish Short Assured Tenancy Agreement (whether it be Furnished House/Flat or Unfurnished House/Flat).

CODE	SF205	
ISBN	1 898217 34 3	10 DIGIT
ISBN	978 1 898217 34 3	13 DIGIT
PRICE	£4.49	

Authors

Ajay Ahuja
The Buy-to-Let Bible
The Seven Pillars of Buy-to-Let Wisdom

Ajay Ahuja is a well-known buy-to-let entrepreneur and founder of the national accountancy practice Accountants Direct. Ajay started with £500. Through buy-to-let, he now has a property portfolio now worth millions.

Joseph Bradshaw
House Buying, Selling and Conveyancing

Joseph Bradshaw was an estate agent and mortgage broker who achieved fame in the 1980s when, from their garage, he and his wife Margaret published a series of books on DIY conveyancing. From the *Financial Times* to *Gardener's Weekly*, his *Guide to House Buying Selling and Conveyancing* made the headlines.

Among the many accolades he earned, his favourite was 'the guru of layperson conveyancing' from *The Times*. The current Lawpack edition is an updated version of Joseph Bradshaw's original.

Kat Callo
Making Sense of Leasehold Property
The Survivor's Guide to Buying a Freehold

Kat Callo is an international strategy consultant, writer and leading advocate of leaseholder rights in England and Wales. She is founding director of Rosetta Consulting, a strategy consultancy that advises leaseholders, solicitors, surveyors, government bodies and other clients on collective enfranchisement, lease extensions, right to manage and related leasehold subjects.

Adam Church
Landlords' Letters

Since graduating from university in 1998, Adam Church has worked extensively in the property industry in the South West of England. He has qualifications from the Guild of Letting and Management and the Association of Residential Letting Agents. He now works mainly from his home in Bristol where he writes full-time and offers independent advice to private landlords of residential tenancies.

Dominic Farrell
The Jet-to-Let Bible

Dominic Farrell is a full-time property investor in the UK and overseas. He is the founder of Bewarethesharks.com, a leading property economics, investment analysis and investor training company. He speaks at property events and trade shows and his views are sought by the national press and television. He also contributes to property investment journals and newspapers.

Howard Gooddie
Buying Bargains at Property Auctions

Howard Gooddie is a freelance auctioneer. Before retirement, he was head of auctions at Longden & Cook Commercial in Manchester, one of the city's oldest firms of Chartered Surveyors.

Howard is well-known as a main contributor to the monthly magazine *Property Auction News*; he also as chairs and is main lecturer at their biannual conference. Armed with his ivory gavel, he now principally performs on the rostrum for Edward Mellor, a firm of estate agents in Manchester and Cheshire.

Roy Hedges
Book-Keeping Made Easy
Running your own Business Made Easy

Roy Hedges currently writes business guides for entrepreneurs and owners of small businesses. He writes from extensive first-hand experience of starting, buying and selling businesses. Besides addressing manufacturing and trade association gatherings and small business forums on various business topics, he has broadcast on BBC Radio Essex.

Henmans Solicitors
Health & Safety at work Essentials

Mary Duncan, Finbar Cahill and Penny Heighway, are specialists in health and safety law at Henmans Solicitors in Oxford. Their expertise derives from Henmans' long-established personal injury practice, which handles claims nationally for both claimants and defendants. Henmans is recognised as a leading personal injury firm in the legal directories.

Yvette Hoskings-James
Business Agreements Made Easy

Yvette Hoskings-James worked as an in-house lawyer for various multinational organisations before setting up a business consultancy. She now provides advice and training workshops on risk management, contracts and business law. Yvette is also a voluntary business mentor through a nationwide voluntary mentoring scheme.

Danny Lee
Buying Property in France

Danny Lee practised as a solicitor until 1990. Since then he has written for national newspapers, such as *The Times* and the *Guardian*, on the law and an array of other subjects.

Authors

Maureen Mullally
DIY Separation & Divorce

Maureen Mullally studied law at King's College, London. She was called to the English Bar at Gray's Inn and to the Irish Bar at King's Inn in Dublin.

She has practised as a barrister specialising in family law for more than 25 years and now works as a writer and mediator in family disputes.

Veronica Newman
Small Claims Guide

Veronica Newman is a barrister and member of Gray's Inn. After private practice at the Bar, she worked for solicitors, first in Manchester and then for a national law firm in Cardiff. Later she was a university lecturer in law, both to students and to professionals. She has now returned to legal practice as a sole practitioner.

Philippa Pearson
Unmarried Couples and the Law

Philippa Pearson specialises in all aspects of family law and is a member of the Resolution National Committee, and the Lord Chancellor's Ancillary Relief Advisory Group.

She writes, lectures and broadcasts on many aspects of family law.

Jon Robins
A Parent's Guide to the Law

Jon Robins has been a legal journalist for seven years, writing for *The Times* and *The Independent*. He is also contributing editor of *The Lawyer* magazine.

Tessa Shepperson
Residential Lettings

Tessa Shepperson is a solicitor in private practice in Norwich. She specialises in residential landlord-and-tenant work.

Melanie Slocombe
DIY Employment Law
Employment Law Made Easy
Your Rights at Work

Melanie Slocombe is a partner in London office of the international law firm McDermott, Will & Emery, where she specialises in employment law.

The Society of Genealogists
Trace your Family Tree Kit

The Society of Genealogists is the UK's leading genealogy research institution. Its London base houses the country's most important genealogy library and provides support and advice for those investigating the lives of past generations.

H M Williams Chartered Accountants
Tax Answers at a Glance
101 ways to pay less tax

H M Williams have clients ranging from multi-million-pound household name organisations to individual taxpayers. In 2001 they won a *Daily Telegraph*/Energis Customer Service Award.

Hugh Williams
Proper Coffee and Other Ways to Grow your Business
Working from Home Pocket Guide
How to Avoid Inheritance Tax
Self-Employment Kit

Hugh Williams qualified as a Chartered Accountant in 1970. He started his own practice H M Williams Chartered Accountants in 1973.

He has held positions on the committee of the Tax Faculty of the Institute of Chartered Accountants and has also addressed the Tax Faculty Conference on tax practice management.

Index

Title	Page
101 Ways to Pay Less Tax Book	22
301 Legal Forms, Letters & Agreements Book	26
Anti-Gazumping Agreement (England & Wales) Form Pack	27
Book-Keeping Made Easy Book	20
Builder/Decorator Contract (England & Wales) Form Pack	27
Business Agreements Made Easy Book	19
Business Letters Made Easy Book	20
Business Partnership Agreement (England & Wales) Form Pack	27
Business Partnership Agreement (Scotland) Form Pack	28
Buying & Selling a Business Made Easy Book	18
Buying Bargains at Property Auctions Book	14
Buying Property in France Pocket Guide Book	17
The Buy-to-Let Bible Book	14
Cohabitation Agreement (England & Wales) Form Pack	27
Employment Contract (England & Wales) Form Pack	28
Employment Contract (Scotland) Form Pack	28
Employment Contracts Kit	9
Employment Law Book	24
Employment Law Made Easy Book	19
Furnished House/Flat Rental Agreement (England & Wales and Scotland) Form Pack	27
General Power of Attorney (England & Wales) Form Pack	28
General Power of Attorney (Scotland) Form Pack	28
Health and Safety at Work Essentials Book	25
Holiday Letting Agreement (England & Wales) Form Pack	28
Holiday Letting Agreement (Scotland) Form Pack	28
House Buying, Selling and Conveyancing Book	15
House/Flat Share Agreement (Non-Resident Owner) (England & Wales and Scotland) Form Pack	27
House/Flat Share Agreement (Resident Owner) (England & Wales and Scotland) Form Pack	27
Household Inventory (England & Wales and Scotland) Form Pack	27
How to Avoid Inheritance Tax Book	21
The Jet-to-Let Bible Book	10
Landlords' Letters Book	12
Last Will & Testament Kit	4
Limited Company Formation Made Easy Book	19
Limited Company Kit	9
Living Will (England & Wales) Form Pack	28
Making Sense of Leasehold Property Book	11
Notice of a Short Assured Tenancy (Scotland) Form Pack	28
Notice to Terminate (England & Wales and Scotland) Form Pack	27
A Parents' Guide to the Law Book	23
Personnel Manager Book	26
Pools Syndicate Agreement (England & Wales) Form Pack	28
Power of Attorney Kit	7
Probate Kit	8
Proper Coffee and Other Ways to Grow your Business Book	25
Ready-Made Company Minutes & Resolutions Book	26
Rent Book	15
Residential Letting Kit	6
Residential Lettings Book	14
Running your own Business Made Easy Book	20
Sales Representative Agreement (England & Wales) Form Pack	28
Self-Employment Kit	9
Sell your own Home Kit	8
Separation & Divorce Book	25
Separation & Divorce Kit	7
The Seven Pillars of Buy-to-Let Wisdom Book	15
Share Certificate (England & Wales) Form Pack	28
Small Claims Book	24
Small Claims Kit	7
Stock Transfer (England & Wales) Form Pack	28
The Survivor's Guide to Buying a Freehold Book	13
Tax Answers at a Glance Book	22
Trace your Family Tree Kit	8
Trip and Slip Book	22
Unfurnished House/Flat Rental Agreement (England & Wales and Scotland) Form Pack	27
Unmarried Couples and the Law Pocket Guide Book	17
Vehicle Purchase Agreement (England & Wales) Form Pack	28
Your Rights at Work Pocket Guide Book	17
Wedding Planner Kit	5
Wills, Power of Attorney & Probate Book	24
Working From Home Pocket Guide Book	16

Lawpack Publishing Limited
76 - 89 Alscot Road
London SE1 3AW

Tel: 020 7394 4040
Fax: 020 7394 4041
Email: enquiries@lawpack.co.uk

www.lawpack.co.uk
0606392